Let's Make Cute Stuff by Aranzi Aronzo!

# Fun Dolls

ARONZ습
ARANZI ARONZO

# Contents

Hi, we're Aranzi Aronzo.
This book contains
instructions on
how to make all kinds of
plush dolls.
Cute ones, weird ones,
slightly scary ones—
all kinds!
Talk to them as
you make them with love.
Give them names
when they're done.
They're your friends
at that point.
Make cute friends
and enjoy your time
together!

**White Rabbit**
Carefree.
She loves to eat,
have fun, and sleep.
Not so good with the
handicrafts. She's best
friends with Brown Bunny.

# Before You Start

**Brown Bunny**
She's a cool, smart, responsible,
and nice girl rabbit.
She has a knack for handicrafts.
She sort of talks like
an old lady, though.
Best friends with White Rabbit.

---

**01** Hi, I'm Brown Bunny.

**02** Heyyy! White Rabbit here.

**03** You can make all kinds of plush dolls by reading this book.

**04** But you might regret it if you don't read these pages first.

---

**05** You'll suffer terribly if you don't read this first? Scary!

**06** Yeah. "Better safe than sorry," as they say.

**07** Got it! I'll read this first because I don't want to have any regrets!

**08** Yeah, you should really read this before you make anything.

---

**09** **Step 1: Materials and Tools**
An explanation of the materials and tools you'll be using frequently

**10** **Scissors**
For cutting patterns, fabrics, felts, and threads.

**Glue**
To glue on eyes, noses, and mouths.
You can use either cloth glue or wood glue.

**11** **Chalk pencils**
Chalk pencils are used to outline your patterns. Use light pencils for dark fabrics and dark pencils for light fabrics so that they stand out.
Chalk pencils are useful because you can erase them even if you mess up. But simple colored pencils will do if you don't have chalk pencils.

**12** You can sew either by hand or with a machine.

**Sewing Needle**
No particular length or thickness required. Use what works best for you.

**If you have one** **Sewing Machine**
If you have a sewing machine at home and know how to use it, we recommend you do. You'll be able to work quickly with nice results.
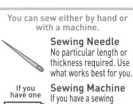

---

**13** **Regular Thread**
Standard No. 60 machine thread. You can also use embroidery threads. These will be used to sew materials like felt that don't stretch. Choose colors close to the fabric color.

**Stretch Thread**
Use No. 50 sewing threads (e.g., polyester or nylon). These threads stretch when you pull. Jersey cloth also stretches when you pull it, so this thread is well suited for it. Choose colors close to the fabric color.

**14** You can use the colors recommended in the "Materials" section or you can use your own favorite colors. Likewise, when it says to use jersey cloth, you can use terry cloth instead. No one will be upset with you.

**Felt**
For things like eyes, noses, and mouths.
**Jersey cloth**
This is stretchable material that feels good against the skin.
**Terry cloth**
This is a soft, 100% cotton fabric that babies especially love.
**Canvas cloth**
A slightly rough cotton fabric. Sturdy, but a little hard to sew.
**Textile cloth**
This is a cotton fabric that will not stretch.

**15** Things you can use to stuff your dolls

**Cotton**
Use to stuff the body and head of your dolls. It's fluffy.

**Pellets**
Use to stuff the body and head of your dolls. They're heavy and give your doll heft.

**Foam Beads**
Small Styrofoam beads that are grainy, crunchy, and light.

---

**16** Things that might be useful to have around

**Awl**
Handy for turning the narrow parts (feet, hands, ears, etc.) right side out.

**Thin, Stick-like Object**
Handy for stuffing the narrow parts with cotton. The tip of a pen, chopsticks, cotton swabs, or anything like that around your house is good.

**17** Things you might use for certain dolls

**Googly Eyes**
The pupils roll around inside. You can just glue them on. They can be found at craft stores.

**Yarn**
To use for things like hair and eyebrows. You can find both thick yarns and thin yarns.

**18** Different projects may call for other materials in addition to these, so check the instructions carefully.

**19** Now that I have the tools and materials, I'm itching to start! I'm going to craft like crazy!

Caution: Don't wave around dangerous tools like White Rabbit is doing here.

# Before You Start

 **Step 2: Patterns**
An explanation of patterns

**20**

---

Each pattern has a cutting line and a sewing line. The space between these two is called the "seam margin." If you enlarge the pattern to the recommended size, the margin will be about 0.5-1.0 cm wide.

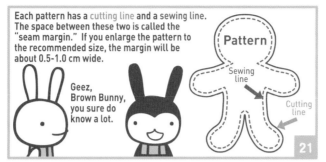

Geez, Brown Bunny, you sure do know a lot.

Pattern

Sewing line

Cutting line

**21**

---

Most patterns need to be enlarged on a copy machine to be at the ideal size. Please enlarge to the ratio recommended on the "Patterns" page for each doll.

Copy machine

**22**

---

You can vary the ratios and make dolls of various sizes. But be careful when you sew, because the seam margins increase or decrease too.

Copy machine

**23**

---

Having the patterns overlap like this is a real pain!

It is, but please trace the patterns onto separate sheets without complaining too much.

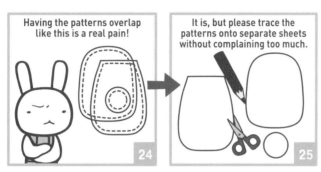

**24**  **25**

---

Once you've enlarged or traced the pattern, please cut it out.

Snip!

**26**

---

Tips on how to sew a clean line
Recommended for those who aren't confident they can sew very neatly.

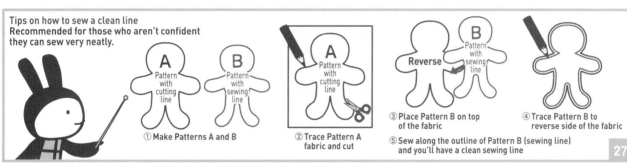

A
Pattern with cutting line

B
Pattern with sewing line

① Make Patterns A and B

A
Pattern with cutting line

② Trace Pattern A fabric and cut

Reverse

B
Pattern with sewing line

③ Place Pattern B on top of the fabric

④ Trace Pattern B to reverse side of the fabric

⑤ Sew along the outline of Pattern B (sewing line) and you'll have a clean sewing line

**27**

---

 **Step 3: Tracing Patterns onto Fabric**
Explanation of how to transfer the patterns you've made onto fabric

**28**

---

Most fabrics have a direction to the grain. The patterns have "grain line" written on them, too. Align the direction of the pattern to the grain of the fabric and trace an outline of the pattern onto the fabric with a chalk pencil.

Width  Grain line  Length

Pattern

Cloth

**29**

---

If you get the grain line wrong, the doll will look kind of weird

Do I look weird?

Stretched

because the fabric may stretch differently lengthwise

**30**

---

This way, 2 pieces
Other way, 2 pieces
4 pieces altogether

In this case, you need the same pattern pointing in opposite directions (symmetry). Trace two patterns using the front side, turn it over, then trace two more using the reverse side. Please read carefully before you trace the patterns.

**31**

---

Awl, grain line, seam margin... I've learned so many new words! I feel smart.

**32**

---

Good for you!

**33**

### Step 4: How to Sew
An explanation of how to sew

**34**

When it says "sew along the dotted line," you can either sew with a machine or by hand. Either way is fine.

**35**

**If you're sewing with a machine**

Sew a straight stitch. A stitch of about 2.5-3.0 mm comes out the most cleanly. (Be careful with stretchy fabrics, because larger seams will look like holes when the fabric stretches.) If you have a sewing machine, you'll be able to work quickly with nice results.

**36**

**If you're sewing by hand**

Do a backstitch or a straight stitch if you sew by hand. With stretchy fabrics, a straight stitch will show holes when the fabric is stretched, so use a backstitch.

1 Out
3 Out   2 In   Backstitch

**37**

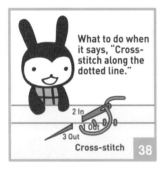

What to do when it says, "Cross-stitch along the dotted line."

2 In
1 Out
3 Out
Cross-stitch

**38**

What does "tacking" mean? Who or what am I tacking? I can't do it! I don't get it!

**39**

"Tacking" means sewing a simple straight stitch before joining pieces of fabric with a final machine- or hand-stitch. "Tacking" first will make your final stitch come out cleaner.

Tack   Remove
Simple straight stitch   Final stitch
Remove tacking thread once final stitching is done

**40**

We aren't tacking dolls to the wall, okay?

That's a relief.

**41**

### Step 5: Insertions
An explanation of how to insert body parts

**42**

This is what you do when it says, "Insert ears between two stacked halves of the body."

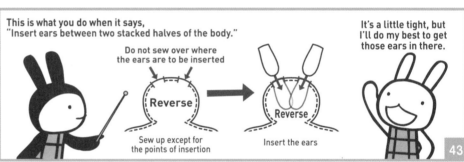

Do not sew over where the ears are to be inserted

Reverse

Sew up except for the points of insertion

Reverse

Insert the ears

It's a little tight, but I'll do my best to get those ears in there.

**43**

### Step 6: Turning Right Side Out
An explanation of how to turn the doll right side out

**44**

Turn the doll right side out from the designated opening.

**45**

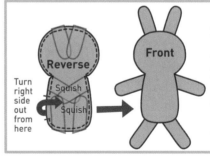

Reverse

Turn right side out from here
Squish
Squish

Front

It's pretty hard to turn a body that's packed with arms and legs right side out. The holes for turning them out are small. Turn them out slowly, part by part, stretching the cloth, pushing from the inside and pulling from the outside.

**46**

Use a pointy object like an awl on long, thin pieces to pull the tips out or turn them right side out.

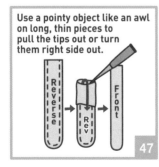

Reverse   Rev   Front

**47**

**Owww, that hurt!**

Blood

**48**

Awls are dangerous. Please be careful when using them.

**49**

You should have said that sooner, Brown Bunny. I just stabbed my finger.

**50**

## Step 4: Shaping the Doll
An explanation of how to shape your doll after it's been turned right side out

**51**

After turning your doll right side out and before stuffing it with cotton, put your hand inside and shape the face and body. If you stuff the doll with cotton without shaping it first, it will look all ragged.

Shape it with your hand.

It'll look lumpy if you don't.

This doll is ragged because it wasn't shaped before being stuffed with cotton. It's still kind of cute, though.

**52**

## Step 8: Stuffing with Cotton
An explanation of how to stuff cotton

**53**

Stuff the cotton in little by little starting with the outer edges. Keep smoothing out the head and body as you're stuffing. Stuff the cotton so that the doll is nice and fluffy.

**54**

If you stuff it with too much cotton, it will turn into a rigid doll.

Sounds strong!

**55**

If you stuff the doll with too little cotton, it will turn into a limp doll.

Sounds weak.

**56**

## Step 9: Making the Face
An explanation of how to make faces

**57**

Put the eyes, nose, and mouth on the face AFTER you've stuffed the head with cotton. If you put them on before it's been stuffed, their positions change as you stuff the head and the face may come out weird.

**58**

The face is the life of a doll, so think about the doll's life and be serious when you make its face.

A serious Brown Bunny

**59**

I'm positive life with a cute face is best.

**60**

## Step 10: Handmade Things Are Fun
Make cute friends, okay?

**61**

When you finish your doll, show it off and make everyone jealous.

Look at what I've got!

**62**

And of course, sleep with it every night.

Zzzz

**63**

Wrap one up real nice and give it to a friend as a present.

Yay! I'm so happy!

**64**

You don't have to use the colors or fabrics suggested in this book. Just have fun making the dolls your own way with what you have handy around the house.

**65**

What's funny is that as long as you don't mind messing up and just keep making the dolls, it'll become so much fun that you won't be able to stop.

**66**

Whether or not it comes out well, it will be your one-in-the-world doll. Of course it'll be cute!

**67**

Make cute friends you'll keep happily ever after!

Good luck! Bye bye!

**68**

Most babies seem to like Towel Dolls, and Towel Dolls like babies too.
Babies like to play goo goo ga ga with the ears and arms and legs.
That's the way babies are with Towel Dolls.
Adults can play goo goo ga ga with Towel Dolls too,
but if they get too serious it looks like they're hurting them.

# How to Make Towel Dolls

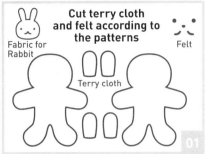

**Cut terry cloth and felt according to the patterns**

Fabric for Rabbit · Terry cloth · Felt

**01**

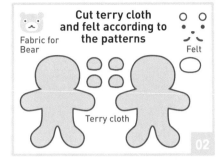

**Cut terry cloth and felt according to the patterns**

Fabric for Bear · Terry cloth · Felt

**02**

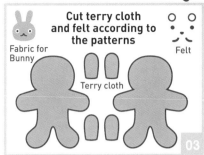

**Cut terry cloth and felt according to the patterns**

Fabric for Bunny · Terry cloth · Felt

**03**

---

**Stack the two halves of the ears inside out and sew along the dotted red line**

Reverse · Reverse · Thread of fabric's color

**04**

**Turn the ears right side out and stuff with cotton**

Reverse · Reverse · Front · Front · Cotton · Stuff

**05**

**Stack the two halves of the body inside out and sew along the dotted red line (Don't sew up the opening or the ear positions)**

Note: The placements for the rabbits' ears and Bear's ears are different

Reverse · Reverse · Reverse · My ears are different! · Thread of fabric's color

**06**

---

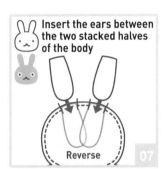

**Insert the ears between the two stacked halves of the body**

Reverse

**07**

**Insert the ears between the two stacked halves of the body**

Reverse

**08**

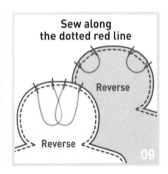

**Sew along the dotted red line**

Reverse · Reverse

**09**

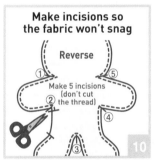

**Make incisions so the fabric won't snag**

Reverse · Make 5 incisions (don't cut the thread)

**10**

---

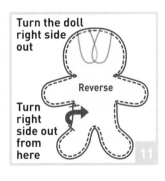

**Turn the doll right side out**

Reverse · Turn right side out from here

**11**

**After you've turned the doll right side out, stuff with cotton and sew shut**

Front · Front · Thread of fabric's color · Cotton

**12**

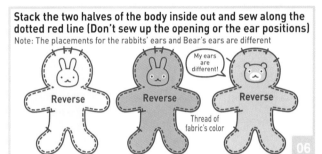

**Position felt eyes, nose and mouth on face**

Their face is their life– make it cute! · Our life depends on this. Make us cute! · Make me the cutest thing on Earth!

**13**

---

**Lightly glue the eyes, nose, and mouth in place, then cross-stitch**

Brown thread · Enlarged view

**14**

**Lightly glue the white of eyes, pupils, nose, and mouth in place, then cross-stitch**

White thread for the whites of eyes · Brown thread for the pupils · Enlarged view · Brown thread

**15**

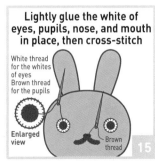

**Lightly glue the white of eyes, pupils, muzzle, nose, and mouth in place, then cross-stitch**

White thread for the white of eyes · Brown thread for the pupils · White thread · Brown thread for the nose and mouth

**16**

I'm Rabbit. · I'm Bear. · I'm Bunny.

**Trio done!**

**17**

# Towel Doll Materials

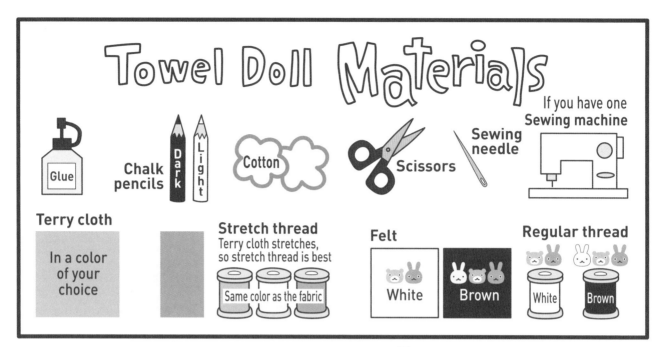

# Towel Doll Patterns

## Enlarge to 125% for the ideal size

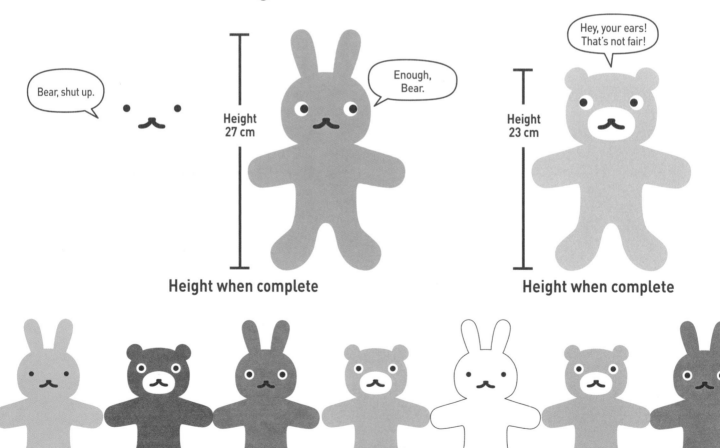

Height when complete

Height when complete

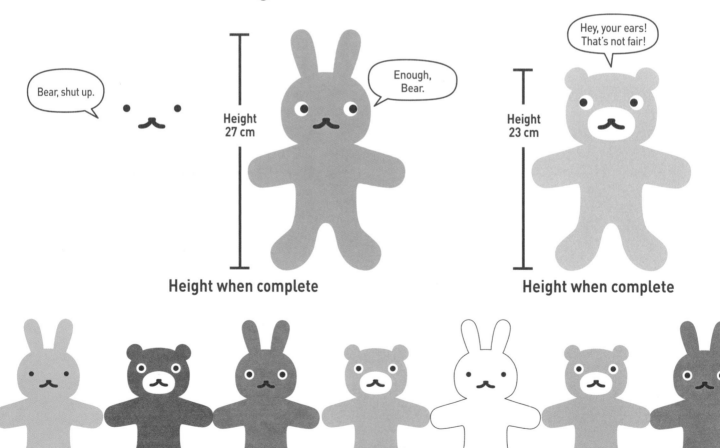

**Have fun with different colors!**

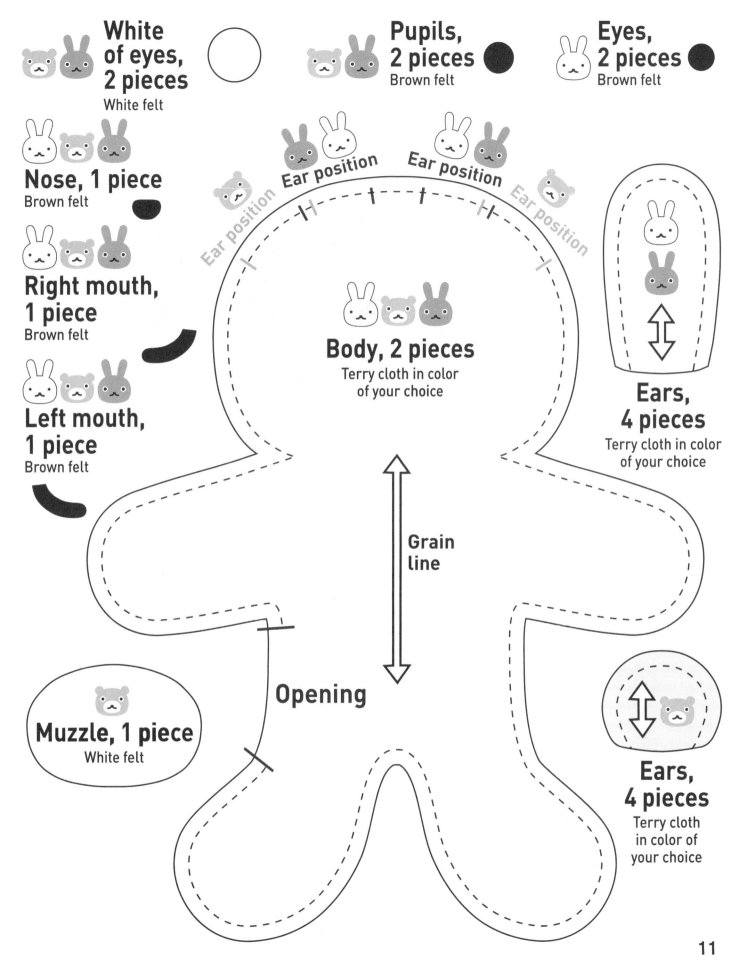

**White of eyes, 2 pieces**
White felt

**Pupils, 2 pieces**
Brown felt

**Eyes, 2 pieces**
Brown felt

**Nose, 1 piece**
Brown felt

**Right mouth, 1 piece**
Brown felt

**Left mouth, 1 piece**
Brown felt

Ear position

Ear position

Ear position

Ear position

Ear position

**Body, 2 pieces**
Terry cloth in color of your choice

**Ears, 4 pieces**
Terry cloth in color of your choice

Grain line

**Opening**

**Muzzle, 1 piece**
White felt

**Ears, 4 pieces**
Terry cloth in color of your choice

11

These are pretty flowers, Rabbity. They sure are, Silky Kay. Really pretty.
Hey Rabbity, which is prettier, me or the flowers?
Umm, I guess the flowers, Silky Kay.
What the? Rabbity, why are you lying? It's not a lie, Silky Kay.
Ugh! Rabbity, that's what's called lying! It isn't Silky Kay. It is, Rabbity.

# How to Make Rabbity Rabbit and Silky Kay

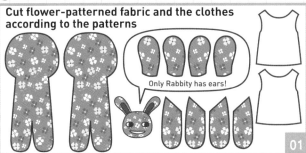

**01** Cut flower-patterned fabric and the clothes according to the patterns

Only Rabbity has ears!

**02** Cut felt according to the patterns

R
K

**03** Stack the halves of the arms inside out and sew along the dotted brown line

Use thread the same color as the predominating color of the pattern

Cotton
Reverse → Front

Turn the arms right side out and stuff with cotton

**04** Stack the halves of the ears inside out and sew along the dotted brown line

Only Rabbity has ears!

Only Rabbity has ears!

Reverse → Front
Cotton

Tokyo girl Rabbity

Turn the ears right side out and stuff with cotton

**05** Only Rabbity has ears!

Reverse

Stack the halves of the body inside out and sew along the dotted brown line

**06** Insert the arms and ears between the two stacked halves of the body

Only Rabbity has ears!

Reverse

**07** Sew along the dotted brown line    Turn right side out

Reverse    Reverse

**08** Stuff with cotton and sew shut

Rabbity    Silky Kay
Front    Front
Cotton

**09** Silky Kay's hair.

① Wrap the yarn around a 5 cm piece of cardboard

Brown yarn

For the top, wrap 50 times

For the sides, wrap 14 times

Note: Depending on the yarn's thickness, vary the number of times you wrap.

② Pull the cardboard out from inside the yarn

Be careful not to let the yarn get tangled

③ Thread the wrapped yarn with a piece of yarn

④ Tie it into a tight knot

⑤ Cut the loop of yarn and you'll get a tuft of hair like this

Brown thread

Squeeze    Squeeze

⑥ Sew the tufts of hair onto the forehead and the sides

**10** Cut the longer strands of hair to give it a nice style

Tokyo girl Silky Kay

It's like a barbershop.

Snip

Snip

**11** Put ribbons around the hair

Long hair, a bob, or braids good too.

Wrap the yarn 4-5 times and tie it tight

Red yarn

Silky Kay's hair looks the same from front or behind

**12** Position the inner ears, white of eyes, pupils, and mouth (only Rabbity has inner ears). Lightly glue them into place, then cross-stitch

Use white thread for the white of eyes and mouth, brown thread for the pupils, and red thread for Rabbity's inner ears

Silky Kay, your face looks really scary.

Rabbity! You're scary, too!

**13** How to make their clothes

With fabric that frays easily, use an overlock or zigzag sewing machine, or sealant to prevent the edges from fraying

① Stack halves inside out and sew along dotted red line

Reverse

Thread of same color as fabric

② Spread pieces out and sew neckline

Reverse

Fold in edge about 5 mm and sew along dotted red line

③ Sew hem of sleeves

Reverse

Fold in edge about 5 mm and sew along dotted red line

④ Stack halves inside out and sew along dotted red line

Reverse

Sew about 5 mm in

⑤ Turn right side out and fold the hem in about 5 mm

Front

⑥ Sew the hem

Front

⑦ Cross-stitch initials on chest

R    K
Rabbity    Silky Kay

Red thread

**14** Done!

R    K

# Rabbity Rabbit and Silky Kay Materials

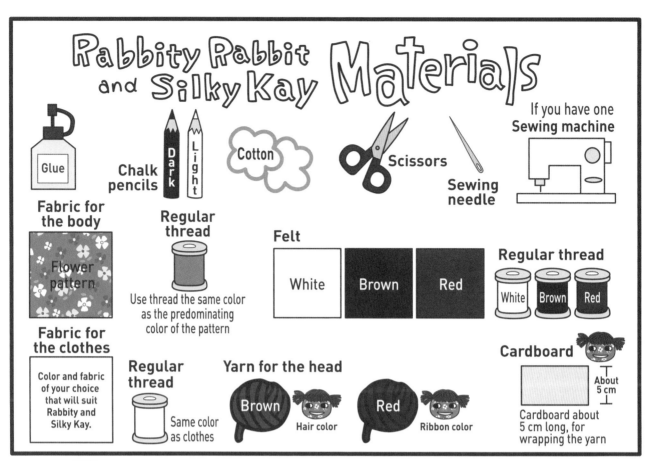

**Glue**

**Chalk pencils** — Dark, Light

**Cotton**

**Scissors**

**Sewing needle**

If you have one **Sewing machine**

**Fabric for the body** — Flower pattern

**Regular thread** — Use thread the same color as the predominating color of the pattern

**Felt** — White, Brown, Red

**Regular thread** — White, Brown, Red

**Fabric for the clothes** — Color and fabric of your choice that will suit Rabbity and Silky Kay.

**Regular thread** — Same color as clothes

**Yarn for the head** — Brown (Hair color), Red (Ribbon color)

**Cardboard** — About 5 cm. Cardboard about 5 cm long, for wrapping the yarn

# Rabbity Rabbit and Silky Kay Patterns

## Enlarge to 125% for the ideal size

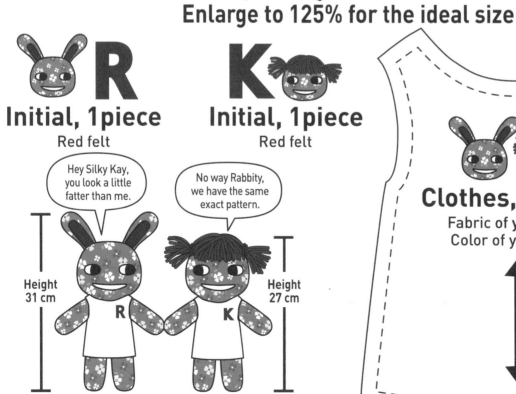

**R** Initial, 1 piece — Red felt

**K** Initial, 1 piece — Red felt

Hey Silky Kay, you look a little fatter than me.

No way Rabbity, we have the same exact pattern.

Height 31 cm

Height 27 cm

**Height when complete**

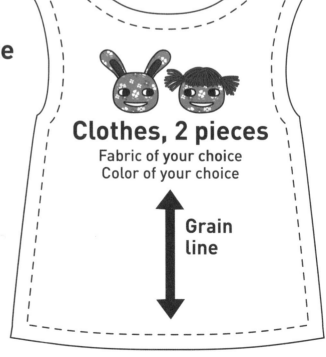

**Clothes, 2 pieces**
Fabric of your choice
Color of your choice

**Grain line**

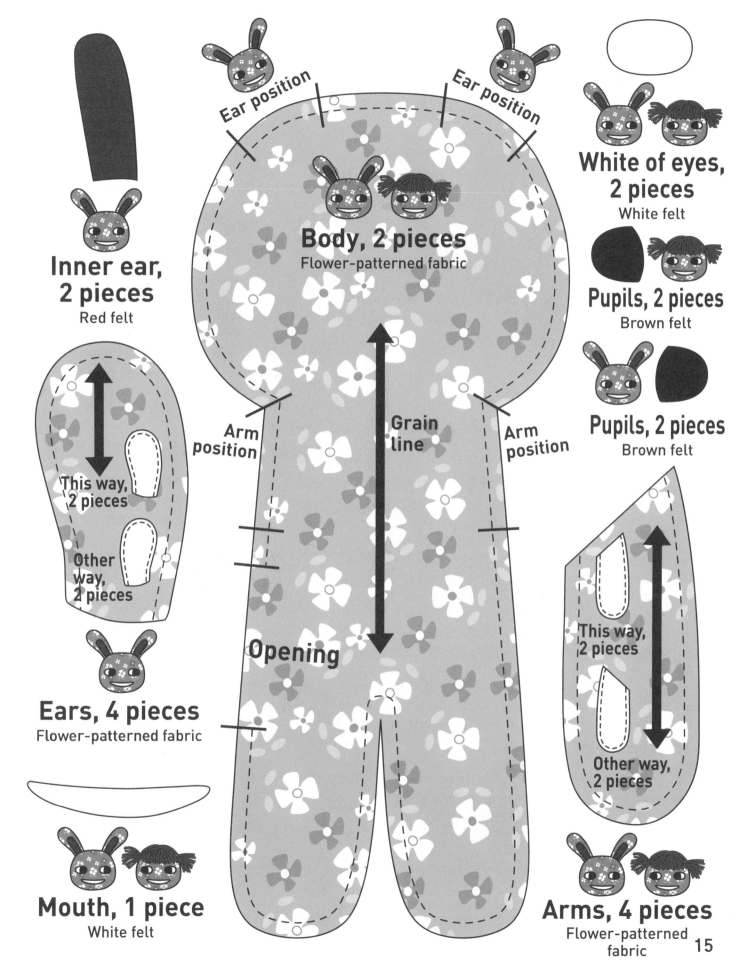

**Inner ear,
2 pieces**
Red felt

**This way,
2 pieces**

**Other
way,
2 pieces**

**Ears, 4 pieces**
Flower-patterned fabric

**Mouth, 1 piece**
White felt

Ear position

Ear position

**Body, 2 pieces**
Flower-patterned fabric

Arm
position

Grain
line

Arm
position

**Opening**

**White of eyes,
2 pieces**
White felt

**Pupils, 2 pieces**
Brown felt

**Pupils, 2 pieces**
Brown felt

**This way,
2 pieces**

**Other way,
2 pieces**

**Arms, 4 pieces**
Flower-patterned
fabric

15

まいぬ
し

He's striped,
so he's called Stripe Dog.
We want you to
remember his name,
so there it is real big
in Japanese.
Have you got it down?

# How to Make Stripe Dog

**Cut jersey cloth according to the patterns**

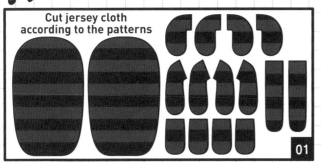

`01`

**Cut felt according to the patterns**

`02`

**Use thread that matches one of the colors of the stripes**

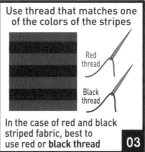

Red thread

Black thread

In the case of red and black striped fabric, best to use red or **black thread**

`03`

---

If you don't have any striped jersey cloth, take jersey cloth in two colors of your choice, cut them into strips, and sew them together to make a striped fabric (though this is kind of a hassle)

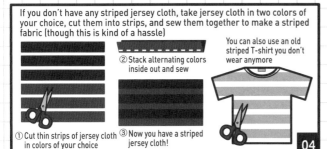

② Stack alternating colors inside out and sew

You can also use an old striped T-shirt you don't wear anymore

① Cut thin strips of jersey cloth in colors of your choice

③ Now you have a striped jersey cloth!

`04`

**Stack the halves of the ears inside out and sew along the dotted white line**

**Turn right side out**
(ears should be floppy so don't stuff with cotton)

`05`

**Stack the halves of the arms inside out and sew along the dotted white line**

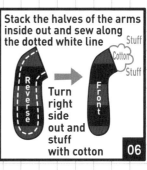

Stuff / Cotton / Stuff

**Turn right side out and stuff with cotton**

`06`

---

**Stack the halves of the legs inside out and sew along the dotted white line**

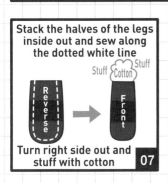

Stuff / Cotton / Stuff

**Turn right side out and stuff with cotton**

`07`

**Stack the halves of the tail inside out and sew along the dotted white line**

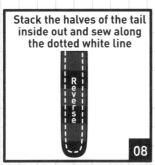

`08`

**Turn right side out and stuff with cotton**

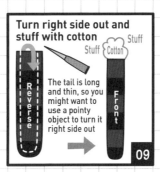

Stuff / Cotton / Stuff

The tail is long and thin, so you might want to use a pointy object to turn it right side out

`09`

**Stack the halves of the body and sew along the dotted white line**

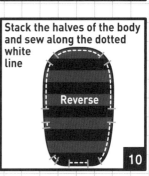

Reverse

`10`

---

**Insert the ears into the halves of the body**

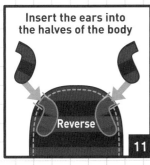

Reverse

`11`

**Sew along the dotted white line**

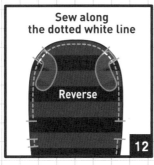

Reverse

`12`

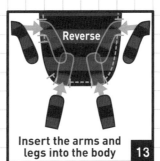

Reverse

**Insert the arms and legs into the body**

`13`

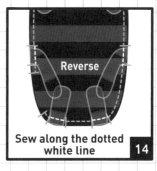

Reverse

**Sew along the dotted white line**

`14`

---

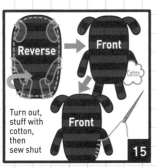

Reverse → Front

Turn out, stuff with cotton, then sew shut

Front

`15`

**Sew on the tail to the backside**

Back

Fold the end of the tail in about 5 mm and sew on

Back

`16`

**Position the white of eyes, pupils, nose, and mouth, lightly glue them into place, then cross-stitch**

White thread for the white of eyes, black thread for the pupils, nose, and mouth

`17`

Woof.

**Done!**

`18`

# Stripe Dog Materials

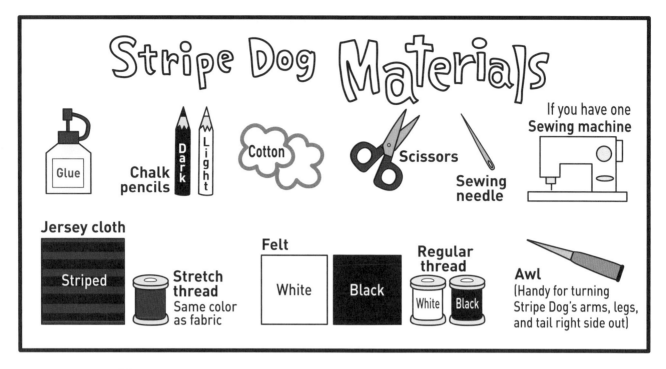

- **Glue**
- **Chalk pencils** — Dark, Light
- **Cotton**
- **Scissors**
- **Sewing needle**
- If you have one **Sewing machine**
- **Jersey cloth** — Striped
- **Stretch thread** — Same color as fabric
- **Felt** — White, Black
- **Regular thread** — White, Black
- **Awl** (Handy for turning Stripe Dog's arms, legs, and tail right side out)

# Stripe Dog Patterns

## Pattern is at 100%, no need to enlarge

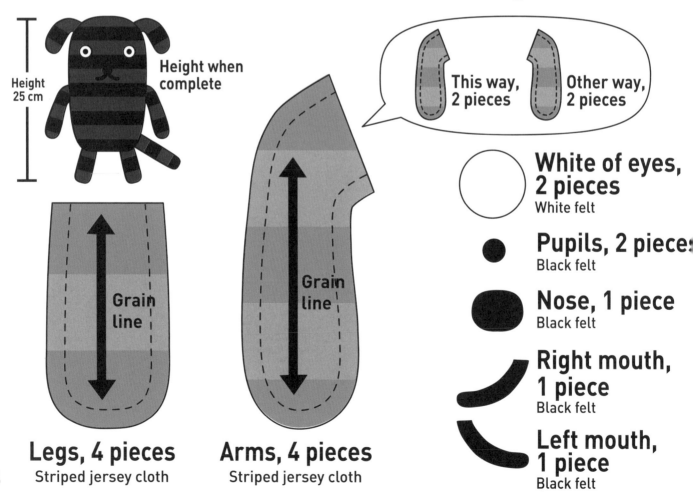

- Height 25 cm — **Height when complete**
- **Legs, 4 pieces** — Striped jersey cloth
- Grain line
- **Arms, 4 pieces** — Striped jersey cloth
- Grain line
- This way, 2 pieces — Other way, 2 pieces
- **White of eyes, 2 pieces** — White felt
- **Pupils, 2 pieces** — Black felt
- **Nose, 1 piece** — Black felt
- **Right mouth, 1 piece** — Black felt
- **Left mouth, 1 piece** — Black felt

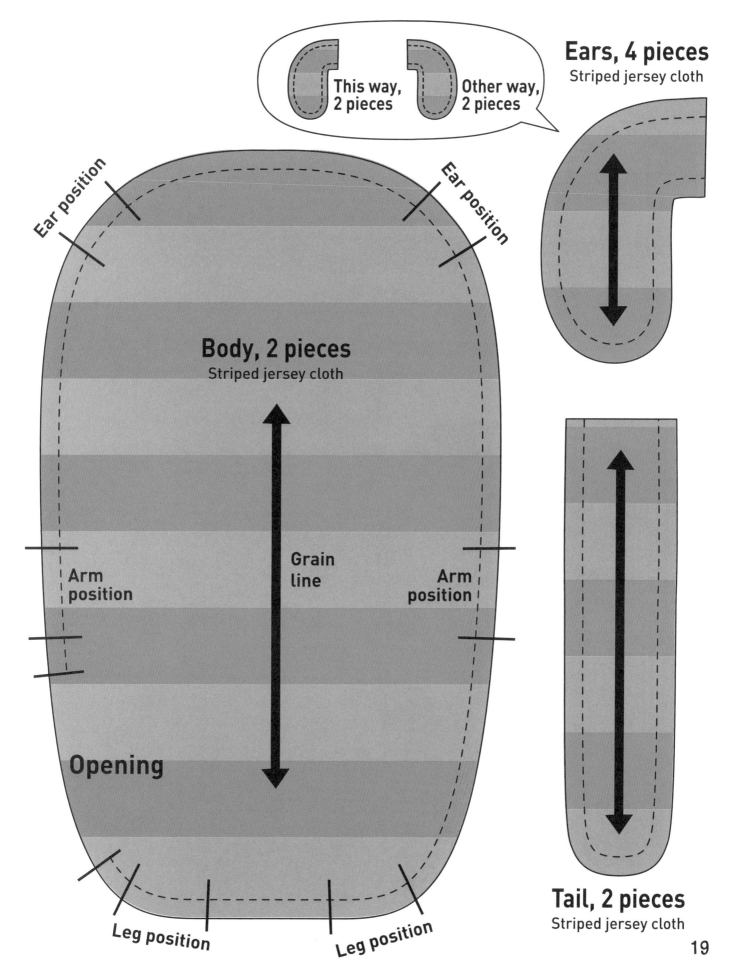

19

I want to be cute,
I want to be cute.
Mr. Cloud, I want to be cute.
Birdies, I want to be cute.
I want to be cuter.
I want to be a lot, lot cuter.

# How to Make Eyelash Bunny

## 01
**Cut fleece according to the patterns**

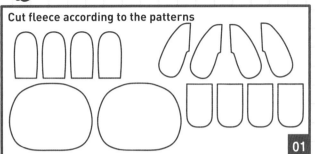

## 02
**Cut cotton fabric according to the patterns**

Clothes

**Cut felt according to the patterns**
- ○○ White of eyes
- ●● Pupils
- ● Nose
- ○○○○ Buttons

## 03
**Position white of eyes, pupils, and nose according to the approximate positions given on the Patterns page**

Patterns page (p. 23)

## 04
**When you've decided where to place the white of eyes, pupils, and nose, make guide marks with a chalk pencil**

Draw the marks about 5 mm inside the actual positions so they can't be seen later

Like this.

## 05
**Straight stitch the eyelashes and mouth with yarn**

Straight stitch

Red yarn

② ①

Make a straight line

Thread the yarn into a doll needle (a long, thick needle)
*The yarn will be easier to thread if you put a little glue on the tip and squeeze it so it's thin enough to thread

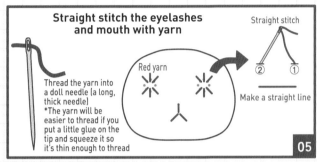

## 06
**Lightly glue the white of eyes and pupils in place, then cross-stitch**

Red thread for the pupils

Pink thread for the white of eyes

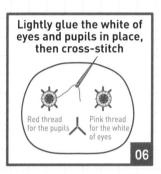

## 07
**Lightly glue the nose in place, then cross-stitch**

Red thread

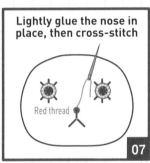

## 08
**Stack the halves of the ear inside out and sew along the dotted red line**

Reverse

Front

White thread

Stuff Cotton Stuff

**Turn the ears right side out and stuff with cotton**

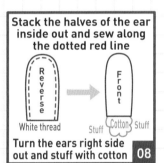

## 09
**Stack the halves of the arms inside out and sew along the dotted red line**

White thread

Reverse

Front

Stuff

Cotton

Stuff

**Turn the arms right side out and stuff with cotton**

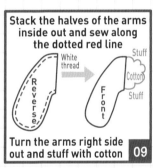

## 10
**Stack the halves of the legs inside out and sew along the dotted red line**

White thread

Reverse

Front

Stuff Cotton Stuff

**Turn the legs right side out and stuff with cotton**

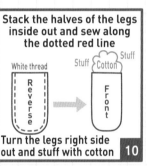

## 11
① Stack halves of face and sew along dotted red line

White thread

Reverse

② Insert the ears between the halves

③ Sew along the dotted red line and turn right side out

White thread

Reverse

④ Stuff with cotton before sewing shut

Front

Stuff Cotton Stuff

White thread

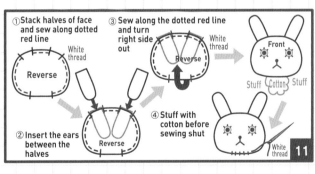

## 12
① Stack halves of the clothes inside out and sew along dotted white line

Reverse

Red thread

② Insert arms and legs between halves

③ Sew along the dotted white line

Reverse

Red thread

Stuff Cotton Stuff

Front

④ Turn out, stuff with cotton, and sew shut

Red thread

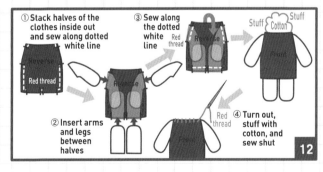

## 13
**Position the buttons and lightly glue into place, then cross-stitch**

Pink thread

## 14
**Sew the head onto the clothing**

White thread

## 15
**Blush the cheeks and ears**
You can apply cloth stencil ink to a sponge brush to get a good red on the cheeks, but regular blush make-up is okay too

Puff Puff Puff Puff

## 16
**Done**

I want to be cuter.

21

# Eyelash Bunny Materials

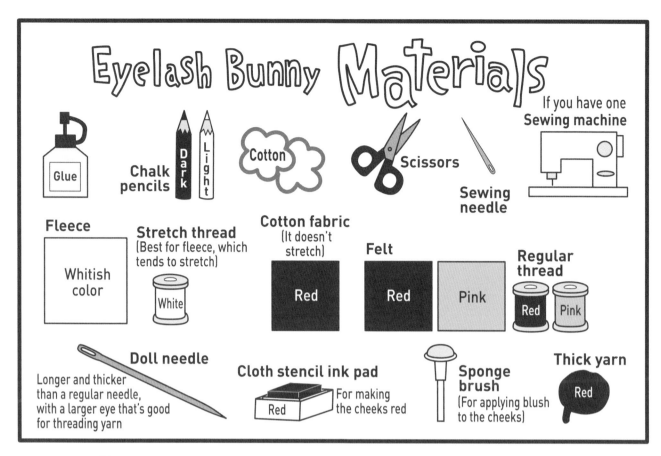

# Eyelash Bunny Patterns

**Enlarge to 125% for the ideal size**

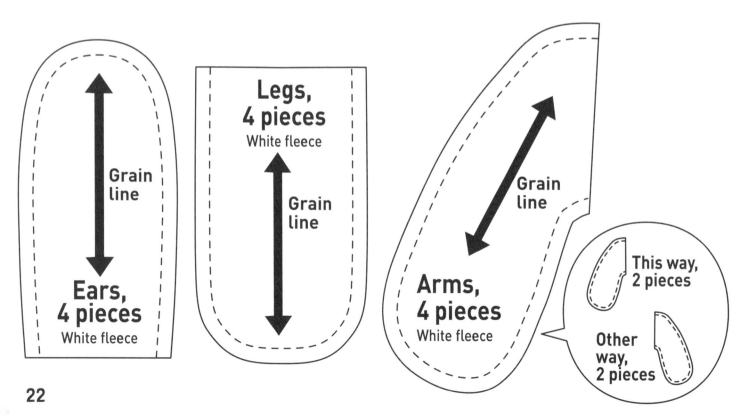

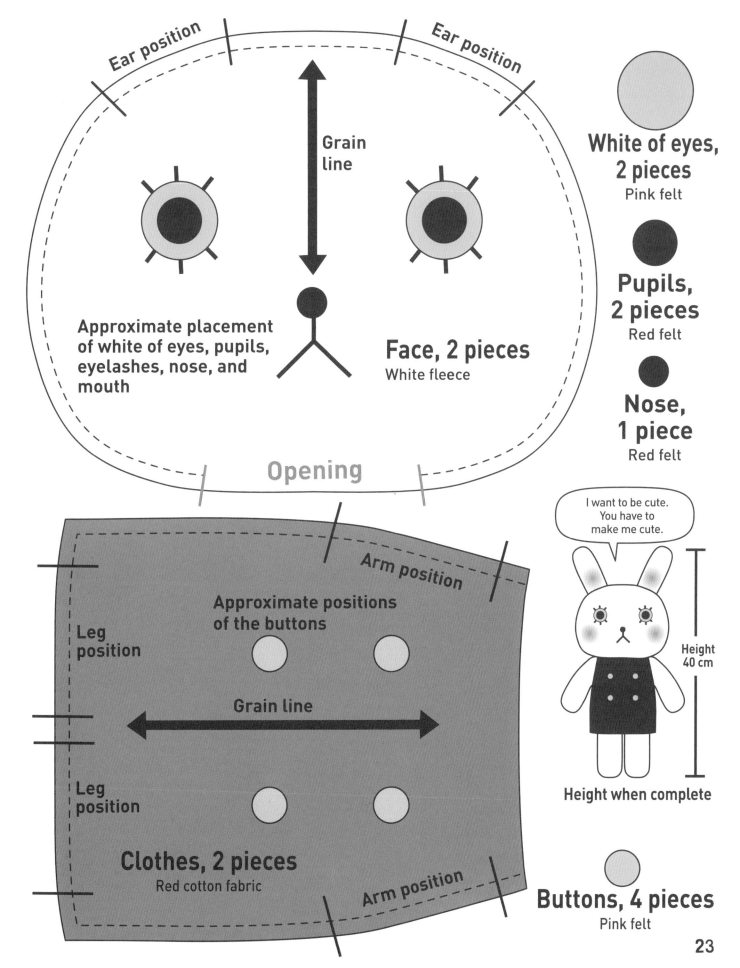

Ear position

Ear position

Grain line

Approximate placement of white of eyes, pupils, eyelashes, nose, and mouth

Face, 2 pieces
White fleece

Opening

White of eyes, 2 pieces
Pink felt

Pupils, 2 pieces
Red felt

Nose, 1 piece
Red felt

I want to be cute. You have to make me cute.

Arm position

Approximate positions of the buttons

Leg position

Grain line

Leg position

Clothes, 2 pieces
Red cotton fabric

Arm position

Height 40 cm

Height when complete

Buttons, 4 pieces
Pink felt

When you shake them,
their arms bounce back and forth, bongo bongo bongo.
That's why they're called Bongo Bear and Bongo Bunny and Bongo Panda.
Not because they're actual drummers or anything.

# How to Make Bongo

 Bear Bunny Panda

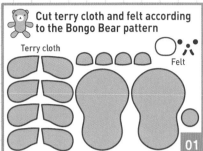
**Cut terry cloth and felt according to the Bongo Bear pattern**
Terry cloth    Felt
`01`

**Cut terry cloth and felt according to the Bongo Bunny pattern**
Terry cloth    Felt
`02`

**Cut erry cloth and felt according to the Bongo Panda pattern**
Terry cloth    Felt
`03`

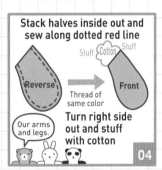
**Stack halves inside out and sew along dotted red line**
Stuff Cotton Stuff
Reverse → Front
Thread of same color
Our arms and legs.
**Turn right side out and stuff with cotton**
`04`

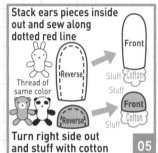
**Stack ears pieces inside out and sew along dotted red line**
Front
Thread of same color
Reverse
Stuff Cotton
Stuff
Front Cotton
Reverse Stuff
**Turn right side out and stuff with cotton**
`05`

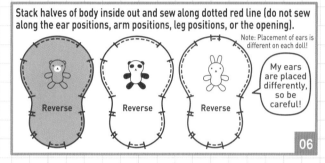
**Stack halves of body inside out and sew along dotted red line (do not sew along the ear positions, arm positions, leg positions, or the opening).**
Note: Placement of ears is different on each doll!
Reverse    Reverse    Reverse
My ears are placed differently, so be careful!
`06`

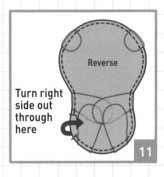
Reverse
Make sure they're the right direction!
**Insert the arms and legs into the halves of the body** `07`

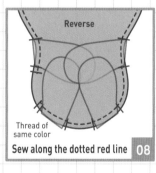
Reverse
Thread of same color
**Sew along the dotted red line** `08`

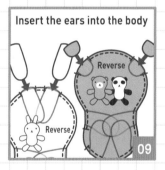
**Insert the ears into the body**
Reverse
Reverse
`09`

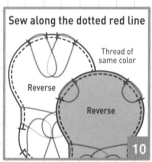
**Sew along the dotted red line**
Thread of same color
Reverse
Reverse
`10`

**Turn right side out through here**
Reverse
`11`

**Once the body's right side out, stuff with cotton and sew shut**
Front → Front
Thread of same color
`12`

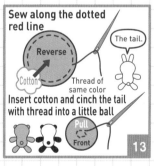
**Sew along the dotted red line**
Reverse
Cotton
Thread of same color
The tail.
**Insert cotton and cinch the tail with thread into a little ball**
Pull Front
`13`

**Sew the tail onto the backside**
Back
Thread of same color
Black thread for Panda.
`14`

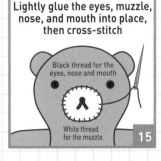
**Lightly glue the eyes, muzzle, nose, and mouth into place, then cross-stitch**
Black thread for the eyes, nose and mouth
White thread for the muzzle
`15`

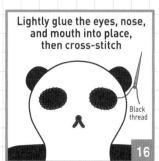
**Lightly glue the eyes, nose, and mouth into place, then cross-stitch**
Black thread
`16`

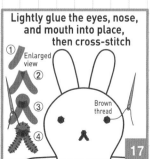
**Lightly glue the eyes, nose, and mouth into place, then cross-stitch**
① Enlarged view
②
③
④
Brown thread
`17`

They drum when you shake them
Bong Bong Bong
Bong Bong Bong
**Bongo Dolls done!**
`18`

25

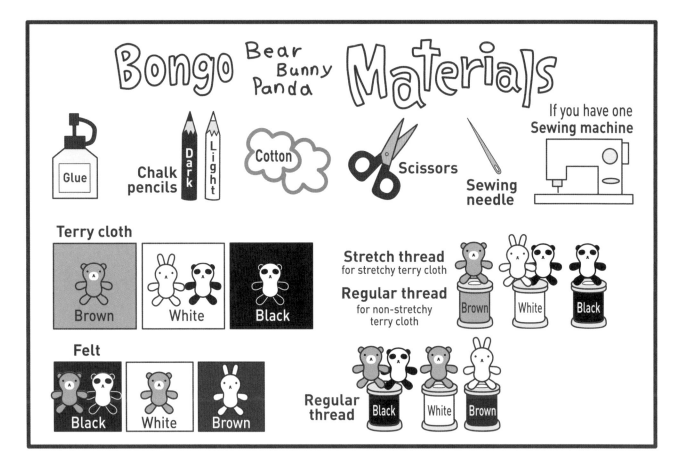

# Bongo Bear Bunny Panda Materials

Glue

Chalk pencils — Dark, Light

Cotton

Scissors

Sewing needle

If you have one Sewing machine

**Terry cloth**
- Brown
- White
- Black

**Stretch thread** for stretchy terry cloth
**Regular thread** for non-stretchy terry cloth
- Brown
- White
- Black

**Felt**
- Black
- White
- Brown

**Regular thread**
- Black
- White
- Brown

# Bongo Bear Bunny Panda Patterns

## Pattern is at 100%, no need to enlarge

**Eyes, 2 pieces**
Black felt

**Eyes, 2 pieces**
Brown felt

**Eyes, 2 pieces**
Black felt

**Nose, 1 piece**
Black felt

**Nose, 1 piece**
Brown felt

**Muzzle, 1 piece**
White felt

Right mouth. Left mouth.

**Right mouth and left mouth, 1 piece each**
Black felt

**Right mouth and left mouth, 1 piece each**
Brown felt

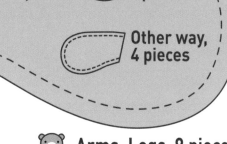
This way, 4 pieces

Other way, 4 pieces

**Arms, Legs, 8 pieces**
Brown terry cloth

**Arms, Legs, 8 pieces**
White terry cloth

**Arms, Legs, 8 pieces**
Black terry cloth

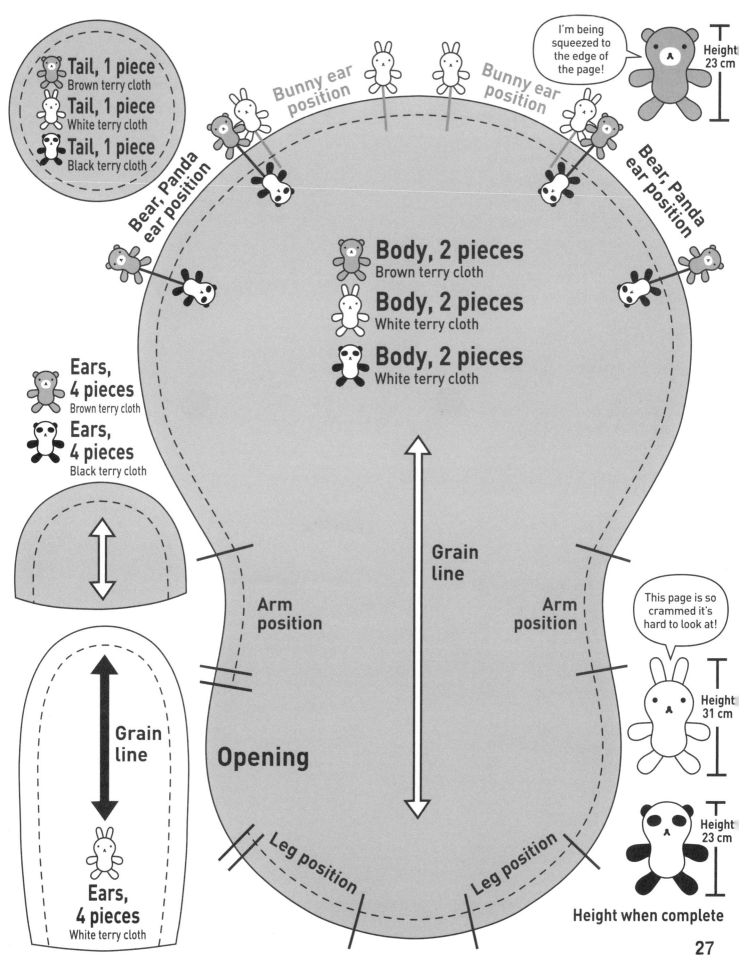

Tail, 1 piece
Brown terry cloth

Tail, 1 piece
White terry cloth

Tail, 1 piece
Black terry cloth

I'm being squeezed to the edge of the page!

Height 23 cm

Bunny ear position

Bunny ear position

Bear, Panda ear position

Bear, Panda ear position

Bear, Panda ear position

Body, 2 pieces
Brown terry cloth

Body, 2 pieces
White terry cloth

Body, 2 pieces
White terry cloth

Ears, 4 pieces
Brown terry cloth

Ears, 4 pieces
Black terry cloth

Grain line

Arm position

Arm position

This page is so crammed it's hard to look at!

Height 31 cm

Grain line

Opening

Ears, 4 pieces
White terry cloth

Leg position

Leg position

Height 23 cm

Height when complete

27

Pig used to be fat until quite recently.
But Pig walked down a long, straight road
and lost some weight.
He's no longer fat. More like medium-sized.
If you want to lose weight too,
you should also walk down
a long, straight road, oink.

# How to Make Pig

## 01
**Cut jersey cloth according to the patterns**

## 02
**Cut felt according to the patterns**

Oink.

## 03
**Cut striped jersey cloth according to the pattern**

Use a striped jersey cloth that suits Pig. Actually, if it suits him, it doesn't even have to be striped.

## 04
**Stack the two halves inside out and sew along the dotted red line**

Reverse → Reverse → Front
Stuff
Cotton
Stuff
Flesh-colored thread
**Turn right side out and stuff with cotton**
Ears, oink.

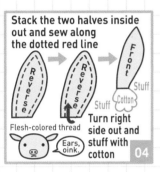

## 05
**Stack the halves inside out and sew along the dotted red line**

Reverse
Flesh-colored thread
Body, oink.

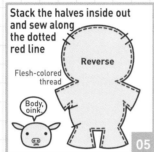

## 06
**Insert the ears into the body and sew along the dotted red line**

Flesh-colored thread
Reverse
Reverse

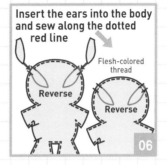

## 07
**Attach the hooves onto the arms and legs. Sew them into the front of the body**

Rev — Front
Rev — Back
Rev
Put hooves on the arms and legs, oink.
Sew approx. 3 mm inside
Flesh-colored thread

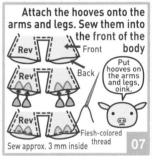

## 08
**Place soles and palms inside out into the openings of the legs and arms. Sew around the circumference.**

Rev / Reverse
Flesh-colored thread
Rev / Reverse / Reverse
Jersey cloth stretches, so don't pull while you sew.
Tack before the final stitch
Sew approx. 5 mm inside

## 09
**Make incisions so the fabric doesn't snag**

Reverse
Make 8 incisions (don't cut the thread)
① ② ③ ④ ⑤ ⑥ ⑦ ⑧

## 10
**Turn the body right side out, fill with cotton, and sew shut**

Turn right side out through here
Cotton
Stuff / Stuff / Stuff
Flesh-colored thread

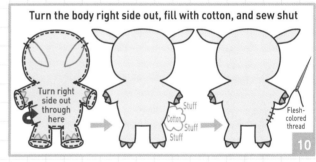

## 11
① Fold the nose fabric in half so that it is inside out
Front
② Sew along the dotted red line
Reverse
Flesh-colored thread
③ The inside-out nose is now a ring
Reverse
Nose, oink.
④ Sew the top of the nose onto the ring you just made, along the circumference
Reverse
Reverse
⑤ Turn the nose right side out
Reverse / Reverse
Sew about 5 mm in
⑥ Stuff with cotton
Front / Front
Reverse / Reverse
Tack before the final stitch
Stuff / Cotton / Stuff

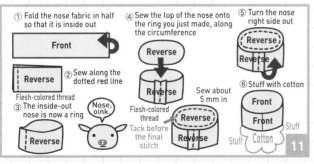

## 12
**Fold the base of the nose in about 5 mm and sew onto the face**

Front / Front
From the side it'll look like this, oink.
Flesh-colored thread

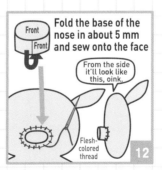

## 13
**Position the eyes, nostrils, and mouth**

Black thread for the eyes and mouth
Pink thread for the nostrils

**Lightly glue them in place, then cross-stitch.**

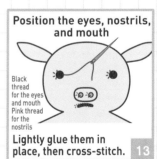

## 14
**How to make the clothes**

With fabric that frays easily, use an overlock or zig-zag stitch, or sealant to prevent the edges from fraying

① Stack the front and back of the clothing pieces inside out and stitch along the dotted red line
Reverse
Thread should be color of one of the stripes
② Open up the pieces and sew the neckline
Reverse
Sew along dotted red line about 5 mm in
Clothes, oink.
③ Sew the sleeve hems
Reverse
Sew along dotted red line about 5 mm in
④ Stack front and back inside out and sew along dotted red line
Reverse
About 5 mm
⑤ Turn out and fold in hem about 5 mm
Front
Front
⑥ Sew the hem

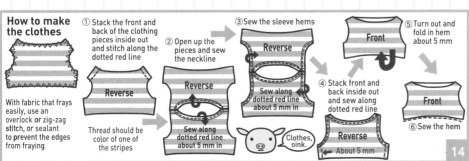

## 15
Tight clothes, oink. Kinda hip, oink.

**Done!**

29

# Pig Materials

- **Glue**
- **Chalk pencils** (Dark, Light)
- **Cotton**
- **Scissors**
- **Sewing needle**
- **Sewing machine** — If you have one
- **Jersey cloth**: Flesh-colored, Striped
- **Stretch thread**: Flesh-colored — Color of one of the stripes of Pig's clothes
- **Felt**: Black, Pink
- **Regular thread**: Black, Pink

# Pig Patterns

**Enlarge to 125% for the ideal size**

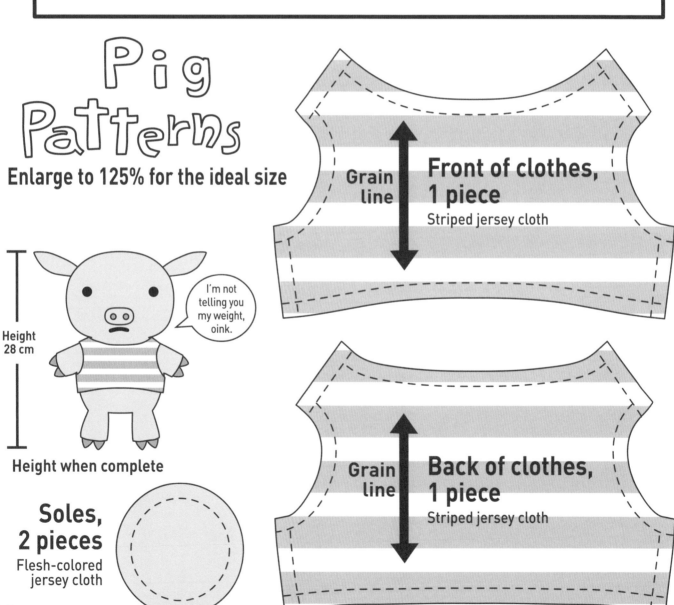

Height 28 cm
Height when complete

I'm not telling you my weight, oink.

**Soles, 2 pieces**
Flesh-colored jersey cloth

**Grain line**

**Front of clothes, 1 piece**
Striped jersey cloth

**Grain line**

**Back of clothes, 1 piece**
Striped jersey cloth

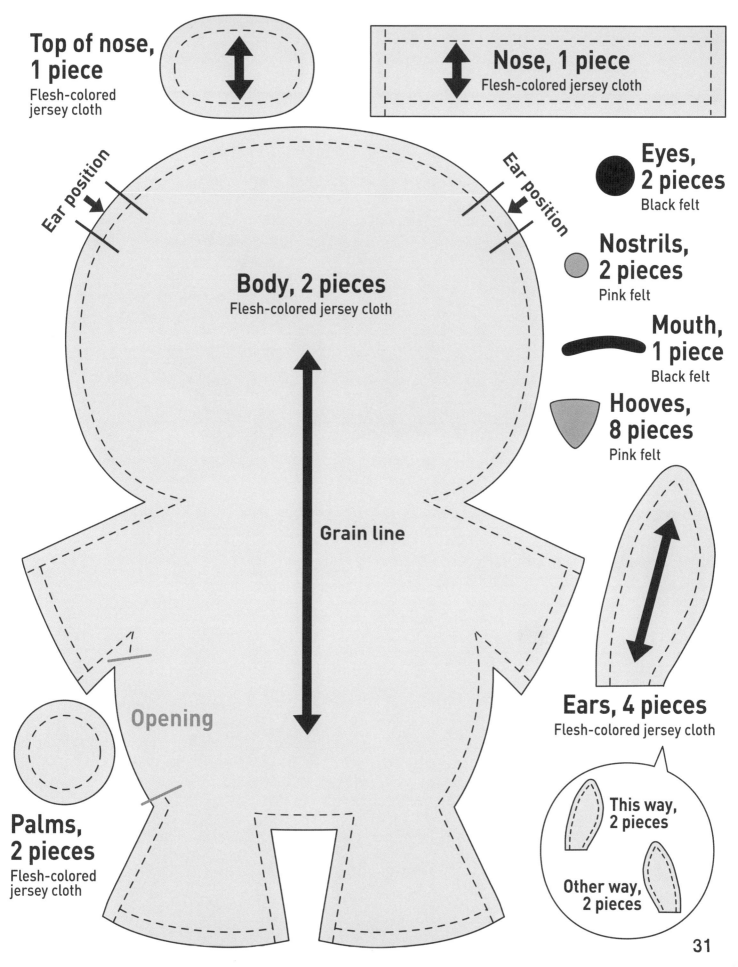

**Top of nose, 1 piece**
Flesh-colored jersey cloth

**Nose, 1 piece**
Flesh-colored jersey cloth

Ear position

Ear position

**Body, 2 pieces**
Flesh-colored jersey cloth

Grain line

Opening

**Eyes, 2 pieces**
Black felt

**Nostrils, 2 pieces**
Pink felt

**Mouth, 1 piece**
Black felt

**Hooves, 8 pieces**
Pink felt

**Ears, 4 pieces**
Flesh-colored jersey cloth

This way, 2 pieces

Other way, 2 pieces

**Palms, 2 pieces**
Flesh-colored jersey cloth

Lamb wants to live with everyone,
living alone is lonely, baa.
I want friends, baa.
Ah, baa, I'm so lonely.
So very lonely, baa baa.
(This is so sad. Let's make Lamb lots of friends.)

### Cut canvas according to the patterns

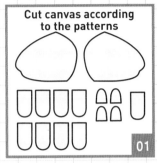

**01**

### Cut faux fleece according to the patterns

**02**

### Cut felt according to the patterns

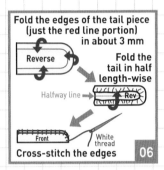

Don't lose my tiny nose, baa.

**03**

### Stack the halves of the legs inside out and sew along the dotted red line

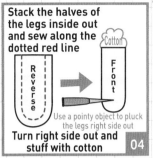

Use a pointy object to pluck the legs right side out

**Turn right side out and stuff with cotton**

**04**

### Fold in the edges of the ear pieces about 3 mm

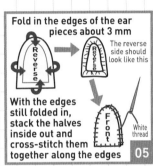

The reverse side should look like this

With the edges still folded in, stack the halves inside out and cross-stitch them together along the edges

Front / White thread

**05**

### Fold the edges of the tail piece (just the red line portion) in about 3 mm

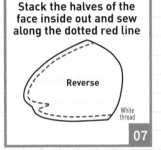

Reverse

Fold the tail in half length-wise

Halfway line — Rev

Front / White thread

**Cross-stitch the edges**

**06**

### Stack the halves of the face inside out and sew along the dotted red line

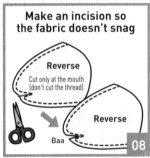

Reverse

White thread

**07**

### Make an incision so the fabric doesn't snag

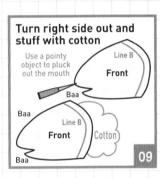

Reverse

Cut only at the mouth (don't cut the thread)

Reverse

Baa

**08**

### Turn right side out and stuff with cotton

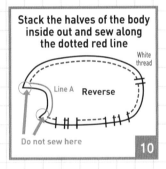

Use a pointy object to pluck out the mouth

Line B / Front / Baa

Baa

Line B / Front / Cotton

Baa

**09**

### Stack the halves of the body inside out and sew along the dotted red line

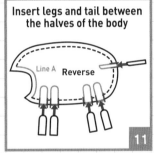

White thread

Line A / Reverse

Do not sew here

**10**

### Insert legs and tail between the halves of the body

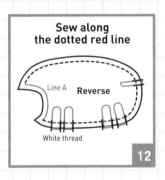

Line A / Reverse

**11**

### Sew along the dotted red line

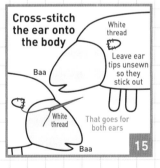

Line A / Reverse

White thread

**12**

### Turn right side out and stuff with cotton

Line A / Front

Cotton

**13**

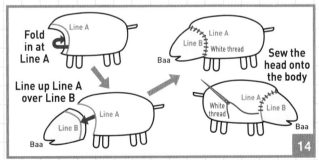

**Fold in at Line A**

Line A

**Line up Line A over Line B**

Line A / Line B / Baa

Line A / Line B / White thread / Baa

**Sew the head onto the body**

White thread / Line A / Line B / Baa

**14**

### Cross-stitch the ear onto the body

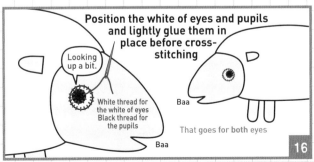

White thread

Baa

Leave ear tips unsewn so they stick out

White thread

That goes for both ears

Baa

**15**

### Position the white of eyes and pupils and lightly glue them in place before cross-stitching

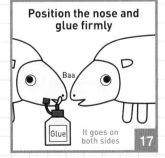

Looking up a bit.

White thread for the white of eyes
Black thread for the pupils

Baa

That goes for **both** eyes

**16**

### Position the nose and glue firmly

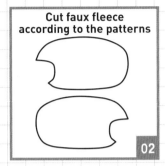

Baa

Glue

It goes on both sides

**17**

### Done

Baa / Baa / Baa / Baa / Baa / Baa

Make a lot for a whole flock!

**18**

# Lamb Materials

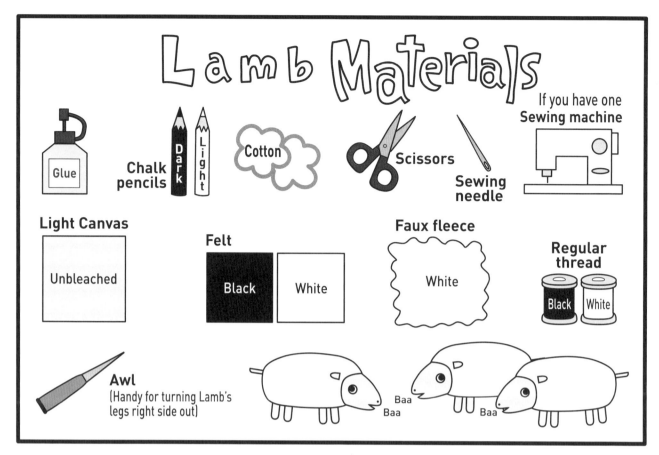

Glue

Chalk pencils — **Dark** **Light**

Cotton

Scissors

Sewing needle

If you have one
**Sewing machine**

**Light Canvas**
Unbleached

**Felt**
Black | White

**Faux fleece**
White

**Regular thread**
Black | White

**Awl**
(Handy for turning Lamb's legs right side out)

Baa Baa   Baa

# Lamb Patterns

## Pattern is at 100%, no need to enlarge

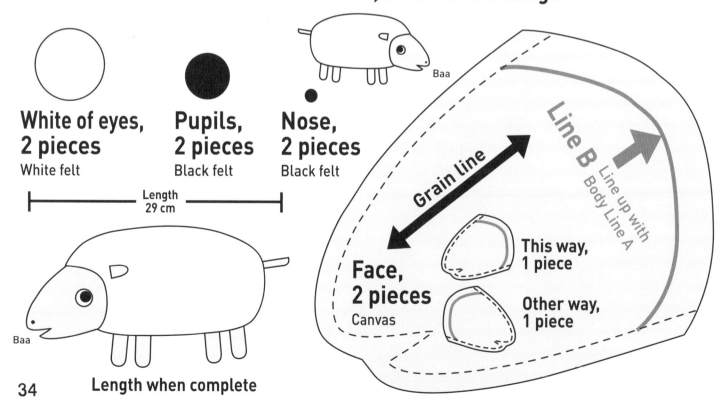

Baa

**White of eyes, 2 pieces**
White felt

**Pupils, 2 pieces**
Black felt

**Nose, 2 pieces**
Black felt

Length 29 cm

**Face, 2 pieces**
Canvas

Grain line

**Line B** Line up with Body Line A

This way, 1 piece

Other way, 1 piece

Baa

**Length when complete**

34

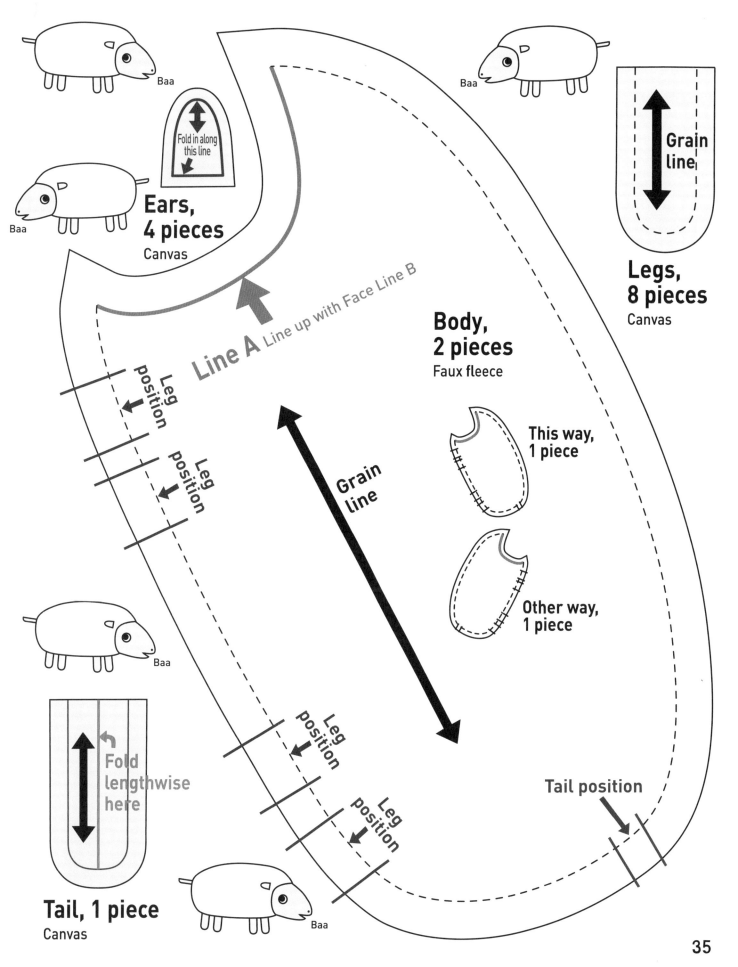

**Ears,
4 pieces**
Canvas

Fold in along
this line

**Legs,
8 pieces**
Canvas

Grain
line

Line A Line up with Face Line B

Leg
position

Leg
position

**Body,
2 pieces**
Faux fleece

Grain
line

This way,
1 piece

Other way,
1 piece

Leg
position

Leg
position

Tail position

Fold
lengthwise
here

**Tail, 1 piece**
Canvas

Baa

35

Ugh... we're totally beat.
We just can't seem to get motivated.
Oh, well.
Are we going to become lazy bums?
I guess it can't be helped.
And why shouldn't we?

### 01
**Cut jersey cloth according to the patterns**

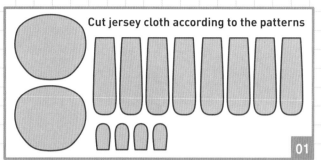

### 02
**Cut felt according to the patterns**

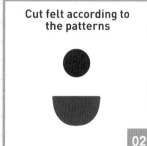

### 03
**Cut clothes fabric according to the pattern**

### 04
**Stack the arms and legs inside out and sew along the dotted red line**

Thread of fabric's color

Reverse | Reverse

**Turn the arms and legs right side out**

The arms and legs are thin, so use a pointy object to pluck the edges out

### 05
**After turning them right side out, put pellets in the arms and legs**

pellets

Front | Front

Do a simple stitch 2-3 mm from the opening to keep the pellets from falling out

### 06
Don't stuff too many pellets in the arms, legs, ears, face, and clothes. We'll look too motivated, and that's not good. Put in just a little so we'll look all floppy and unmotivated.

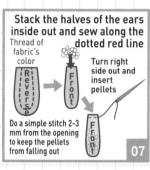

### 07
**Stack the halves of the ears inside out and sew along the dotted red line**

Thread of fabric's color

Reverse | Front

**Turn right side out and insert pellets**

Front

Do a simple stitch 2-3 mm from the opening to keep the pellets from falling out

### 08
**Stack the halves of the face inside out and sew along the dotted red line**

Thread of fabric's color

**Reverse**

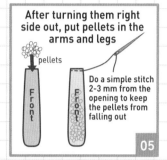

### 09
**Insert the ears between the halves of the face**

**Reverse**

### 10
**Sew along the dotted red line**

Thread of fabric's color

**Reverse**

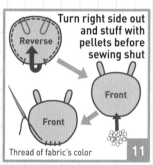

### 11
**Turn right side out and stuff with pellets before sewing shut**

Reverse

Front

Front

Thread of fabric's color

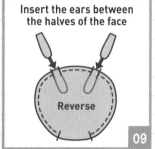

### 12
**Stack the halves of the clothes inside out and sew along the dotted red line**

**Reverse**

Thread of color similar to fabric's

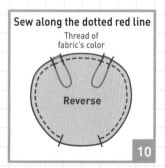

### 13
Insert arms

**Reverse**

**Insert arms and legs between stacked halves of clothes**

Insert legs

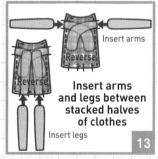

### 14
**Sew along the dotted red line**

Thread of color similar to fabric's

**Reverse**

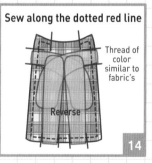

### 15
**Turn right side out and stuff with pellets before sewing shut**

Reverse

Front | Front

Thread of color similar to fabric's

### 16
**Sew the face onto the clothes**

Thread of color similar to jersey cloth

### 17
**Position googly eyes and glue on firmly**

Glue

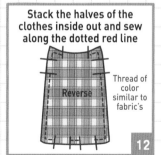

### 18
**Position nose and mouth and glue on firmly**

Glue

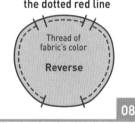

### 19
**Done**

Don't be unmotivated. Make the effort and craft us! But we'll just go on being unmotivated. That's how it is sometimes.

# Unmotivated Kid Materials

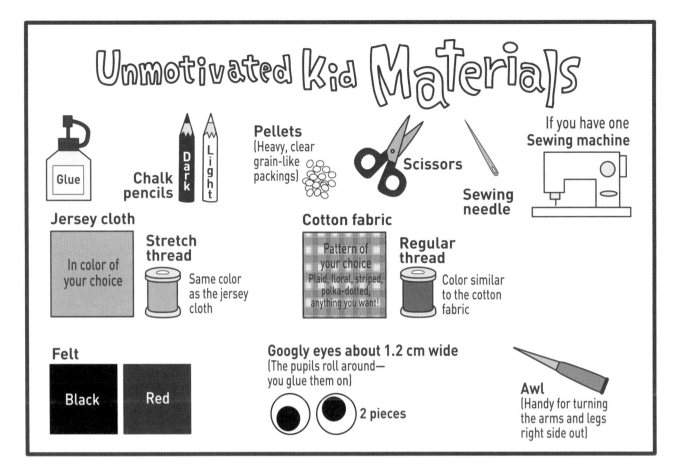

# Unmotivated Kid Patterns

## Pattern is at 100%, no need to enlarge them

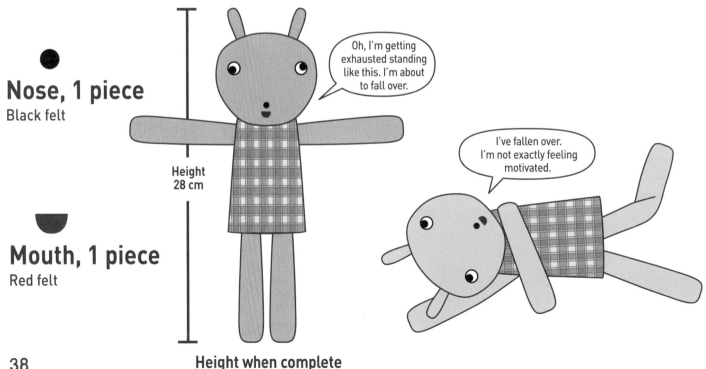

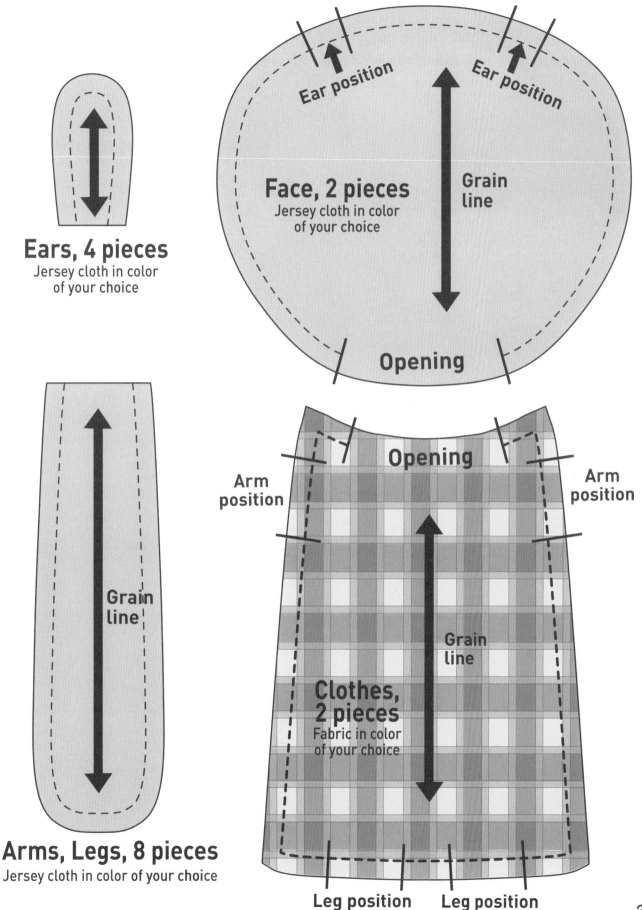

**Ears, 4 pieces**
Jersey cloth in color
of your choice

Ear position

Ear position

**Face, 2 pieces**
Jersey cloth in color
of your choice

Grain
line

Opening

**Arms, Legs, 8 pieces**
Jersey cloth in color of your choice

Grain
line

Opening

Arm
position

Arm
position

Grain
line

**Clothes,
2 pieces**
Fabric in color
of your choice

Leg position

Leg position

Good day. My name is Donkey.
Fine weather we're having today.
This here is a wasteland.
I am traveling alone.
No, I'm not lonely.
Please do not worry about me.

# How to Make Donkey

### Cut felt according to the patterns

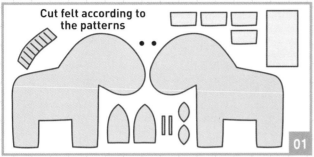

**01**

### Cut mane along the red lines

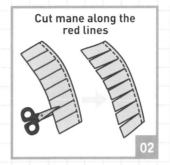

**02**

### Place the mane along the indicated position on Donkey's body and sew along the dotted red line

Light brown thread

Sew about 3 mm in

Front of body

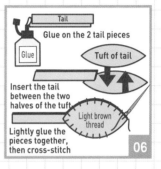

**03**

### Fold the ear pieces in half lengthwise and sew along the dotted red line

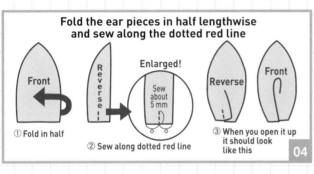

Front
Reverse!!

**Enlarged!**
Sew about 5 mm

Reverse    Front

① Fold in half
② Sew along dotted red line
③ When you open it up it should look like this

**04**

### Place the ears in their indicated positions on the body and sew along the dotted red line

Put the two ears together with the fronts facing out

Front

Sew about 3 mm in

Light brown thread    Front

Front of body

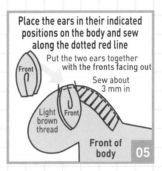

**05**

Tail
Glue on the 2 tail pieces

Glue

Tuft of tail

Insert the tail between the two halves of the tuft

Light brown thread

Lightly glue the pieces together, then cross-stitch

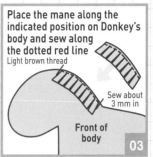

**06**

### Place tail at the indicated position and sew along the dotted red line

Sew about 3 mm in

Front of body    Light brown thread

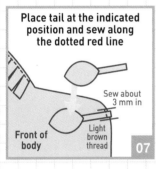

**07**

### Stack the other half of the body on top

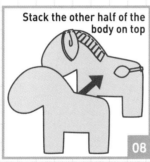

**08**

### With the ears, mane, and tail sandwiched between the two halves of the body, sew along the dotted red line

Light brown thread

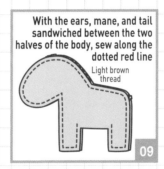

**09**

### Make incisions to keep the fabric from snagging

④

① 
② ③

4 incisions (don't cut the thread)

**10**

### Turn right side out, stuff with cotton, and sew shut

Front

Reverse

Cotton

Front

Light brown thread

For narrow parts like the legs, use a pointy object to turn out neatly

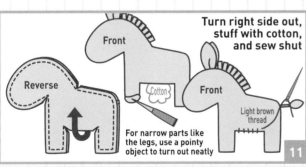

**11**

### Stack the two halves of the hooves together and sew along the dotted red line

Blue thread

Reverse

**Flip right side out**

Reverse

Front

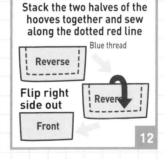

**12**

### Put the hooves on Donkey

Sew just enough of the hooves on so that they don't slip off

Thank you very much.

Blue thread

**13**

### Drape the saddle over Donkey

Sew just enough so that it doesn't fall off

Blue thread

Thank you very much.

**14**

### Position the eyes and lightly glue in place, then cross-stitch

Black thread

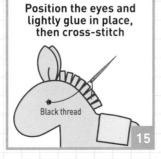

**15**

### Draw the mouth with a pen

Sew in eye and draw mouth on other side too

**16**

Thank you for making me carefully.

If you make him carefully, Donkey will be thankful.

**Done**

**17**

41

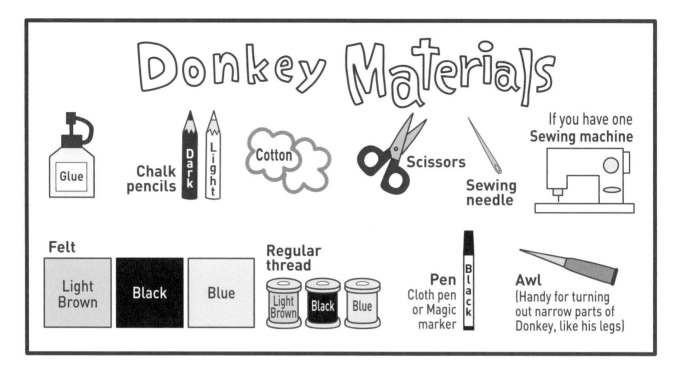

# Donkey Materials

- **Glue**
- **Chalk pencils** (Dark, Light)
- **Cotton**
- **Scissors**
- **Sewing needle**
- If you have one **Sewing machine**
- **Felt**: Light Brown, Black, Blue
- **Regular thread**: Light Brown, Black, Blue
- **Pen** Cloth pen or Magic marker (Black)
- **Awl** (Handy for turning out narrow parts of Donkey, like his legs)

# Donkey Patterns

## Enlarge to 125% for the ideal size

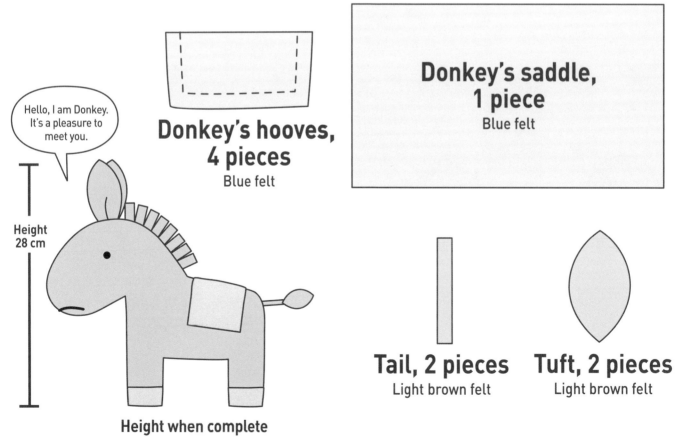

Hello, I am Donkey. It's a pleasure to meet you.

Height 28 cm

Height when complete

**Donkey's hooves, 4 pieces**
Blue felt

**Donkey's saddle, 1 piece**
Blue felt

**Tail, 2 pieces**
Light brown felt

**Tuft, 2 pieces**
Light brown felt

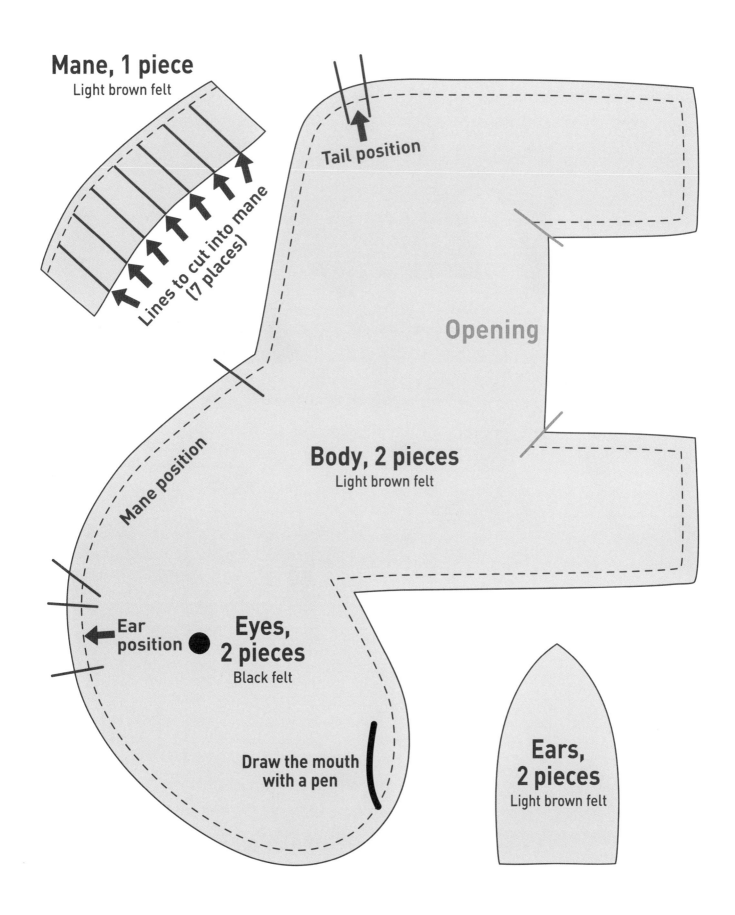

**Mane, 1 piece**
Light brown felt

Lines to cut into mane
(7 places)

Tail position

Opening

Mane position

**Body, 2 pieces**
Light brown felt

Ear
position

**Eyes,
2 pieces**
Black felt

Draw the mouth
with a pen

**Ears,
2 pieces**
Light brown felt

Haha Bunnies are always laughing "Haha!" so they're called Haha Bunnies.
They're looking for lucky four-leaf clovers in the clover field.
"I found some luck! Haha!"
Which one do you think's gotten lucky?

# How to Make Haha Bunnies

**01** Cut a white fabric of your choice according to the patterns, haha

**02** Cut felt according to the patterns too, haha

**03** Stack the halves of the ears inside out and sew along the dotted red line, haha
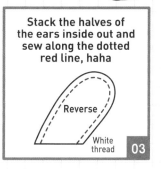
Reverse / White thread

**04** Turn right side out, haha

Reverse / Turn out through here, haha

**05** Stuff with cotton, haha
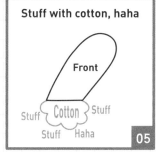
Front / Stuff Cotton Stuff / Stuff Haha

**06** Stack the halves of the tail inside out and sew along the dotted red line, haha

Reverse / White thread

**07** Turn right side out, haha

Reverse / Turn out through here, haha

**08** Stuff with cotton, haha

Front / Stuff Cotton Stuff / Haha Stuff

**09** Stack the halves of the body inside out and sew along the dotted red line, haha
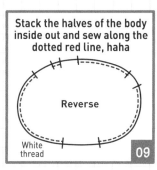
Reverse / White thread

**10** Insert the ears into the body, haha
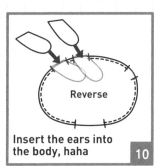
Reverse

**11** Sew along the dotted red line, haha
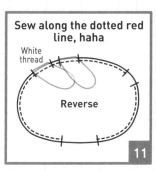
White thread / Reverse

**12** Insert the tail into the body, haha

Reverse

**13** Sew along the dotted red line, haha
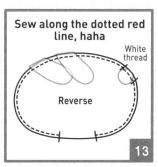
White thread / Reverse

**14** Turn the body right side out, haha
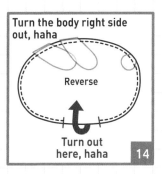
Reverse / Turn out here, haha

**15** Stuff with cotton, haha

Front / Stuff Cotton Stuff / Haha / Front / Sew shut, haha / White thread

**16** Position eyes and mouth, haha Lightly glue in place, then cross-stitch, haha
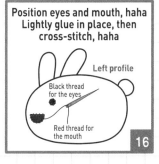
Left profile / Black thread for the eyes / Red thread for the mouth

**17** Position eye, haha Lightly glue in place, then cross-stitch, haha

Right profile / The mouth is on the left side so you don't need to worry about the right side / Black thread

**18** Done, haha

Right profile / Haha / Left profile

**19** Terry cloth Haha Bunnies are soft, haha / Faux fleece Haha Bunnies are cozy, haha

Haha / Haha

45

# Haha Bunny Materials

# Haha Bunny Patterns

## Pattern is at 100%, no need to enlarge

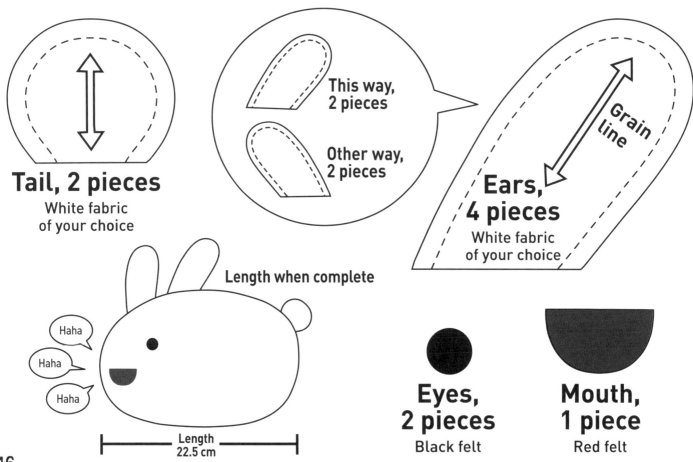

**Tail, 2 pieces**
White fabric of your choice

This way, 2 pieces

Other way, 2 pieces

**Ears, 4 pieces**
White fabric of your choice

Grain line

Length when complete

Length 22.5 cm

**Eyes, 2 pieces**
Black felt

**Mouth, 1 piece**
Red felt

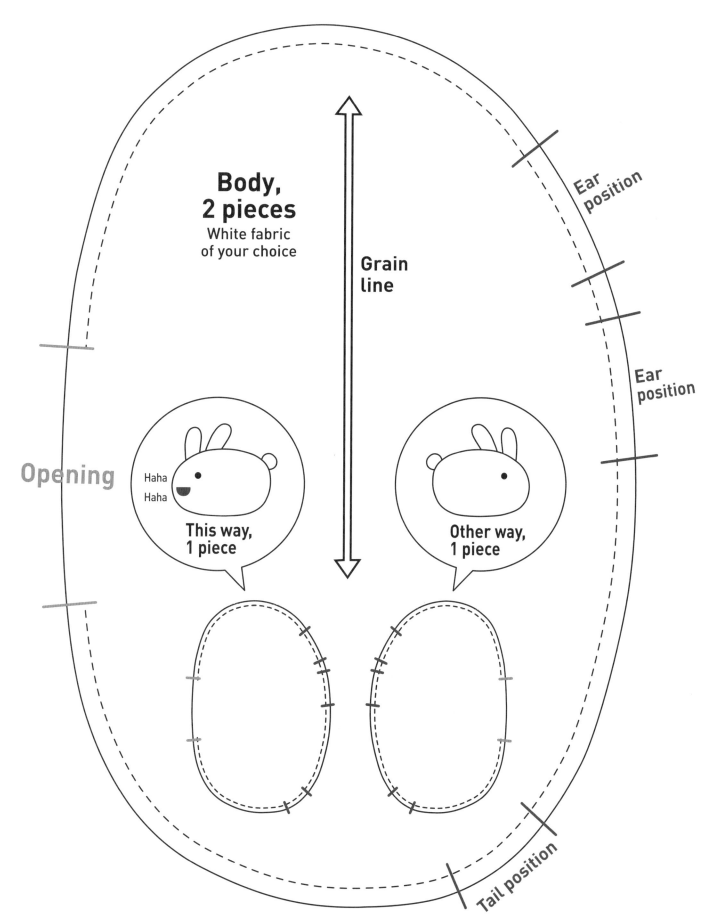

I wrote a song for my Red Bird.
"My cute Red Bird, why do you cry 'chirp chirp'?
Chirp chirp, because I'm hungry!
My cute Red Bird, why are you flying away?
Chirp chirp, I'm flying home for my meal!
Chirp chirp, chirp chirp, see you tomorrow!"

# How to Make Red Birds

### 01
**Cut jersey cloth according to the patterns**

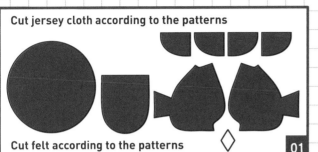

**Cut felt according to the patterns**

### 02
**Sew face along the dotted white line. Place cotton inside and cinch the thread to make a ball**

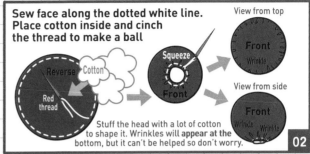

View from top — Front, Wrinkle

View from side — Front, Wrinkle, Wrinkle

Reverse, Cotton, Squeeze, Front, Red thread

Stuff the head with a lot of cotton to shape it. Wrinkles will appear at the bottom, but it can't be helped so don't worry.

### 03
**Stack body side halves inside out and sew along the dotted white line**

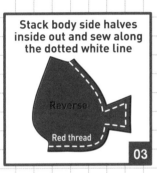

Reverse — Red thread

### 04
**Make incisions so the fabric doesn't snag**

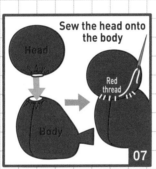

Reverse — 2 incisions (don't cut the thread) ① ②

### 05
① Open body side

② Overlap open body side on body front inside out at the center points and sew along the dotted white line

③ Turn right side out — Through here

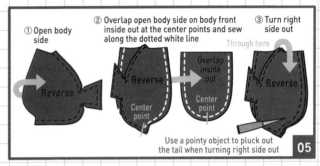

Reverse / Reverse, Center point / Overlap inside out, Center point / Reverse

Use a pointy object to pluck out the tail when turning right side out

### 06
**Sew top of body about 5 mm in, stuff with cotton and pellets, and cinch**

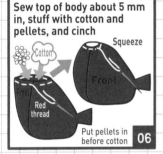

Cotton, Squeeze, Front, Red thread

Put pellets in before cotton

### 07
**Sew the head onto the body**

Head / Red thread / Body

### 08
**Don't worry about the wrinkles between the head and body**

Wrinkle, Wrinkle

It'll look like a little old lady Red Bird, but don't worry about it

### 09
**Stack halves of wings inside out, sew along dotted white line, and turn right side out**

Red thread, Reverse → Reverse

**Fold in the end about 5 mm and sew shut**

Front → Red thread, Front

### 10
**Sew the wings onto the sides of the body**

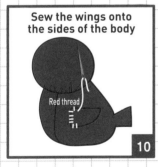

Red thread

### 11
① Fold the beak in half
② Pinch hard to make a crease in the beak — Squeeze
③ It'll look like a beak once it has a crease

### 12
① Position the beak on the head — Front view

② Open up the beak and sew along the dotted red line (the beak's center) — Yellow thread

③ The beak is done — Side view

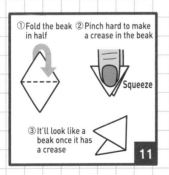

### 13
① Position the **googly** eyes on the head

② Glue them firmly in place — Front view — Glue

③ The eyes are done — Side view

### 14
Done ♪

### 15
If you're seeking happiness, **make a blue bird**

Blue Bird of Happiness

If you're seeking tons of happiness, make tons of blue birds

# Red Bird Materials

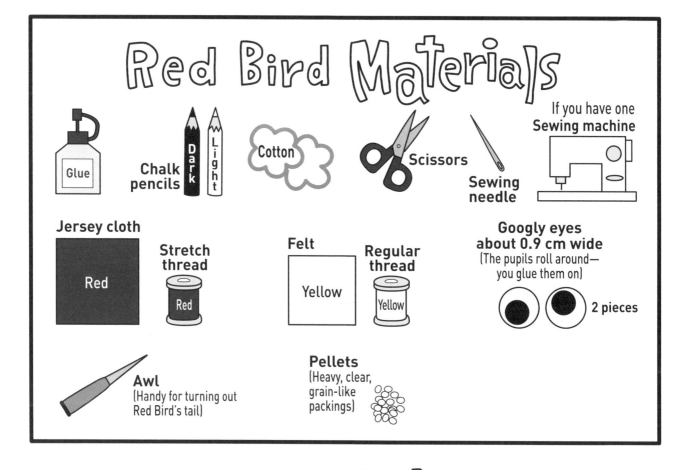

Glue

Chalk pencils — Dark, Light

Cotton

Scissors

Sewing needle

If you have one
Sewing machine

Jersey cloth — Red

Stretch thread — Red

Felt — Yellow

Regular thread — Yellow

Googly eyes
about 0.9 cm wide
(The pupils roll around—
you glue them on)
2 pieces

Awl
(Handy for turning out
Red Bird's tail)

Pellets
(Heavy, clear,
grain-like
packings)

# Red Bird Patterns

**Pattern is at 100%, no need to enlarge**

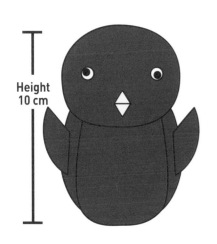

Height
10 cm

**Size when complete**

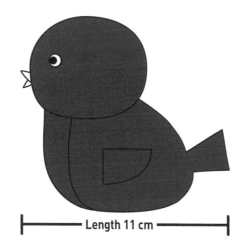

Length 11 cm

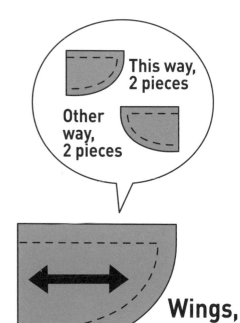

This way,
2 pieces

Other
way,
2 pieces

**Wings,
4 pieces**

Red jersey cloth

**Mouth,
1 piece**

Yellow felt

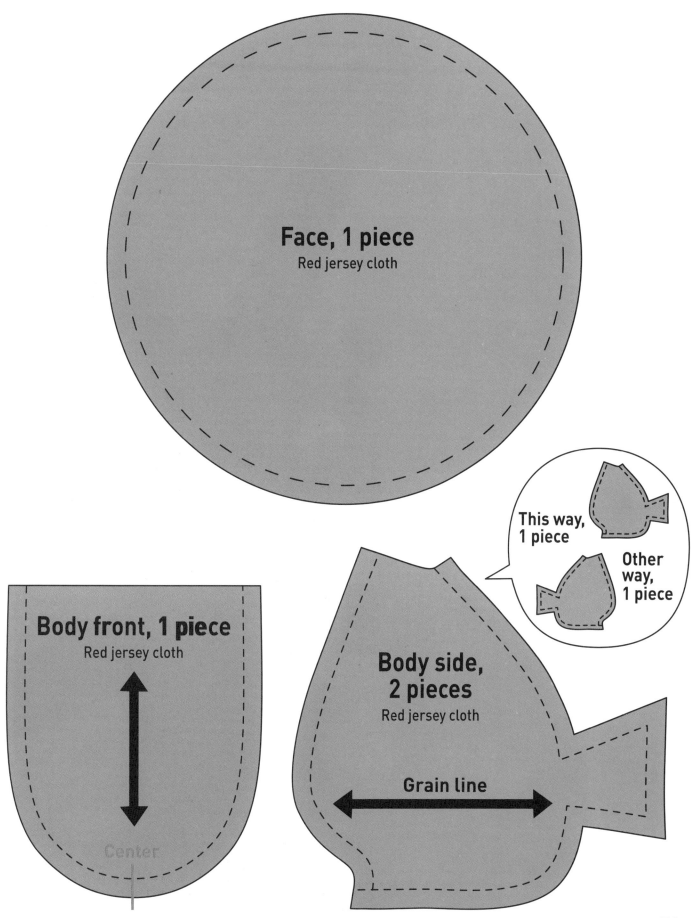

Face, 1 piece
Red jersey cloth

This way, 1 piece

Other way, 1 piece

Body front, 1 piece
Red jersey cloth

Center

Body side, 2 pieces
Red jersey cloth

Grain line

51

"Hey, move your foot. It's been hurting me for a while."
"Oh, I'm sorry. You don't have to get all upset about it."
Haha Rolleyes always look like they're smiling,
but they get angry, too.

# How to Make Haha Rolleyes

### Cut cotton fabric according to the patterns

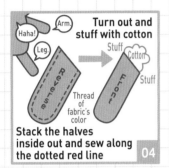

**01**

### Cut felt according to the patterns

Haha!

**02**

### Stack halves inside out and sew along dotted red line

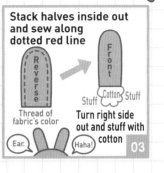

Reverse → Front
Stuff Cotton Stuff
Thread of fabric's color

**Turn right side out and stuff with cotton**

Ear. Haha!

**03**

### Turn out and stuff with cotton

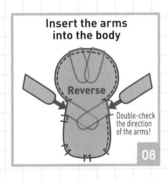

Haha! Arm. Leg.
Stuff Cotton Stuff
Reverse → Front
Thread of fabric's color

**Stack the halves inside out and sew along the dotted red line**

**04**

### Stack the halves inside out and sew along the dotted red line

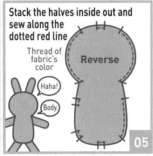

Thread of fabric's color
Reverse
Haha! Body.

**05**

### Insert the ears into the body

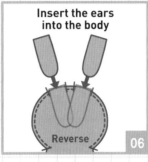

Reverse

**06**

### Sew along the dotted red line

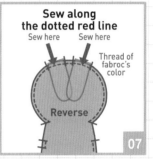

Sew here    Sew here
Thread of fabric's color
Reverse

**07**

### Insert the arms into the body

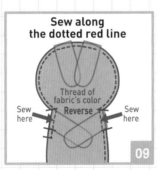

Reverse
Double-check the direction of the arms!

**08**

### Sew along the dotted red line

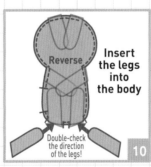

Thread of fabric's color
Sew here    Reverse    Sew here

**09**

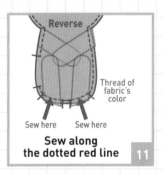

Reverse
**Insert the legs into the body**
Double-check the direction of the legs!

**10**

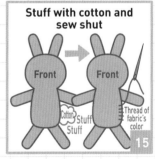

Reverse
Thread of fabric's color
Sew here    Sew here
**Sew along the dotted red line**

**11**

### Make incisions so the fabric doesn't snag

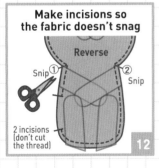

Reverse
Snip ①        ② Snip
2 incisions (don't cut the thread)

**12**

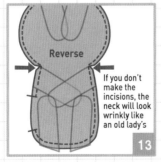

Reverse
If you don't make the incisions, the neck will look wrinkly like an old lady's

**13**

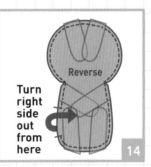

Reverse
**Turn right side out from here**

**14**

### Stuff with cotton and sew shut

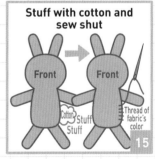

Front → Front
Cotton Stuff Stuff
Thread of fabric's color

**15**

Swirl.    Swirl.
Glue

**Position the googly eyes then glue them firmly in place**    **16**

Swirl.    Swirl.
Haha!    Glue

**Position the mouth and glue it firmly in place**    **17**

Swirl.
Haha!
**Done**

**18**

### Have fun making dolls with eyes and mouths of different sizes

Swirl.
Haha!    Haha!

**19**

53

# Haha Rolleye Materials

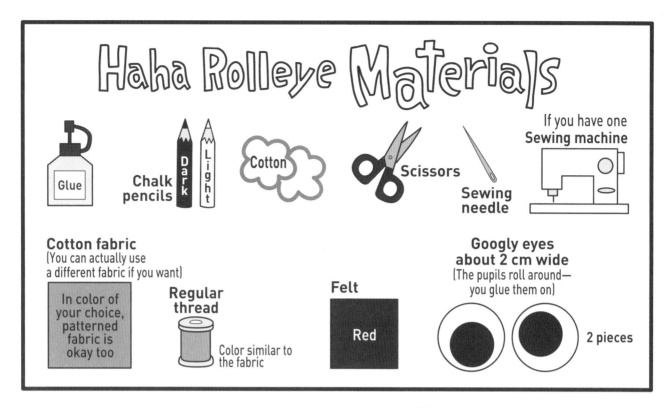

**Glue**

**Chalk pencils** — Dark, Light

**Cotton**

**Scissors**

**Sewing needle**

If you have one
**Sewing machine**

**Cotton fabric**
(You can actually use a different fabric if you want)

In color of your choice, patterned fabric is okay too

**Regular thread**

Color similar to the fabric

**Felt** — Red

**Googly eyes about 2 cm wide**
(The pupils roll around—you glue them on)

2 pieces

# Haha Rolleye Patterns

## Enlarge to 110% for the ideal size

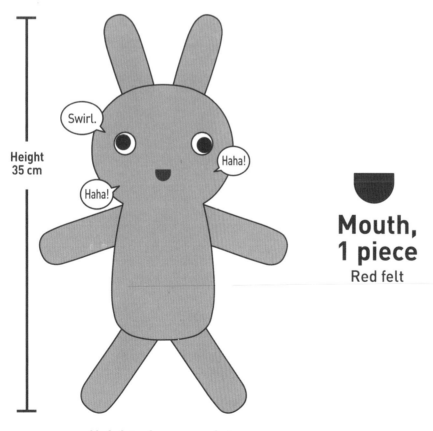

Height 35 cm

Swirl.

Haha!

Haha!

**Height when complete**

Mouth, 1 piece
Red felt

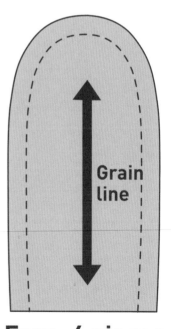

**Grain line**

**Ears, 4 pieces**
Fabric in color of your choice

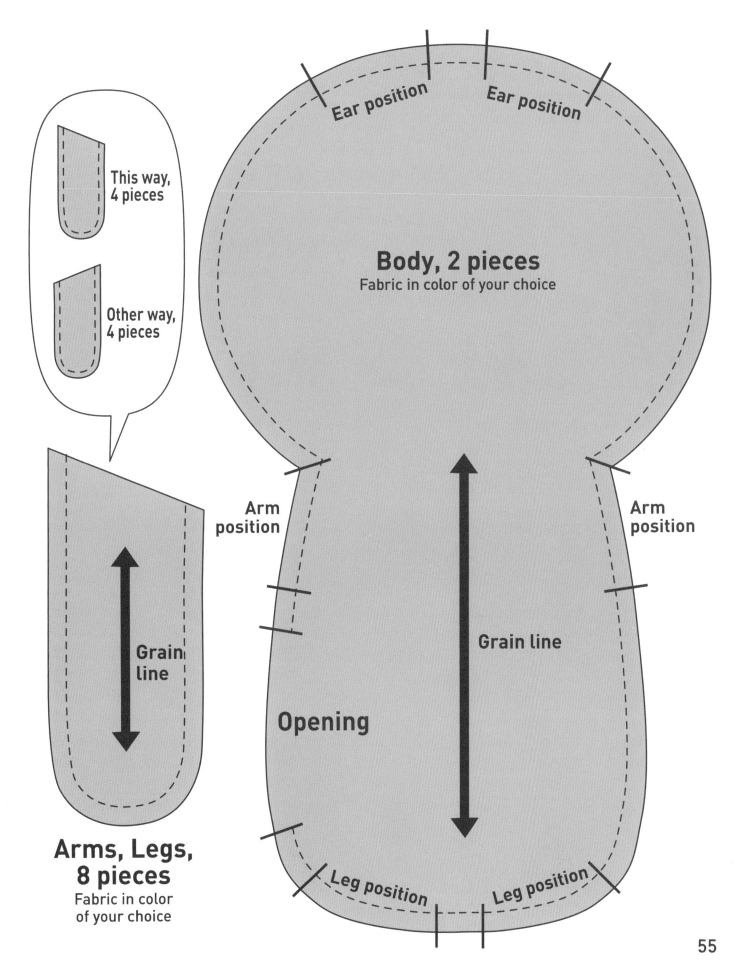

This way, 4 pieces

Other way, 4 pieces

Body, 2 pieces
Fabric in color of your choice

Ear position          Ear position

Arm position          Arm position

Grain line

Grain line

Opening

Arms, Legs, 8 pieces
Fabric in color of your choice

Leg position          Leg position

55

The Turtlies are exhausted.
Turtlies like to climb on top of each other.
Turtlies like to pile up on each other.
It must be heavy for the Turtlie at the bottom.
Poor thing.

# How to Make Turtlies

**01**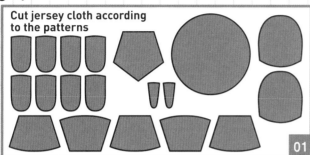
Cut jersey cloth according to the patterns

**02**
Cut felt according to the patterns

Whites of eyes and pupils.

**03**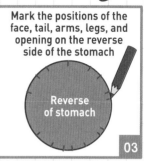
Mark the positions of the face, tail, arms, legs, and opening on the reverse side of the stomach

Reverse of stomach

**04**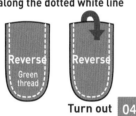
Stack the halves of the arms and legs inside out and sew along the dotted white line

Reverse
Green thread

Reverse

**Turn out**

**05**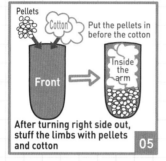
Pellets
Cotton
Put the pellets in before the cotton

Inside the arm

Front

After turning right side out, stuff the limbs with pellets and cotton

**06**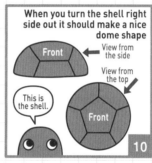
Stack the halves of the face inside out and sew along the dotted white line

Reverse
Green thread

Pellets
Cotton

Front

Turn right side out and stuff with pellets and cotton

**07**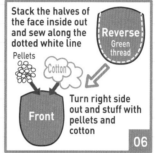
Stack the halves of the tail inside out and sew along the dotted white line

Reverse
Green thread

Pellets
Cotton

Front

Turn the tail right side out and stuff with pellets and cotton

**08**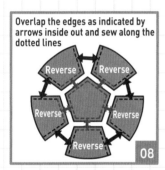
Overlap the edges as indicated by arrows inside out and sew along the dotted lines

Reverse  Reverse
Reverse  Reverse
Reverse

**09**
Be careful when sewing the pieces together

Don't sew all the way to the edge

Leave about 5 mm open

Reverse  Reverse

The secret for making a neat shell.

**10**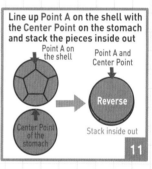
When you turn the shell right side out it should make a nice dome shape

Front
View from the side

View from the top

This is the shell.

Front

**11**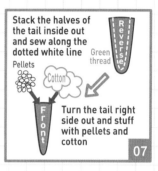
Line up Point A on the shell with the Center Point on the stomach and stack the pieces inside out

Point A on the shell
Point A and Center Point

Reverse

Center Point of the stomach

Stack inside out

**12**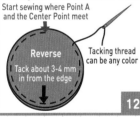
Tack (temporarily straight stitch) the edges of the two stacked pieces starting at Point A and Center Point

Start sewing where Point A and the Center Point meet

Reverse
Tack about 3-4 mm in from the edge

Tacking thread can be any color

**13**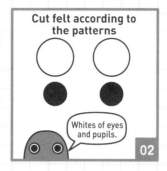
Sew only along the dotted white lines between the position marks you made in **03**
Be careful not to sew over the positions for the face, tail, arms, legs, and opening

Center Point
Reverse of stomach

Green thread
Opening

**14**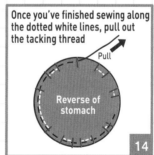
Once you've finished sewing along the dotted white lines, pull out the tacking thread

Pull

Reverse of stomach

**15**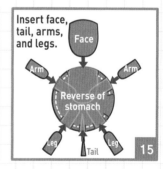
Insert face, tail, arms, and legs.

Face
Arm  Arm
Reverse of stomach
Leg  Leg
Tail

**16**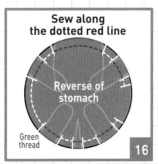
Sew along the dotted red line

Reverse of stomach

Green thread

**17**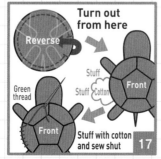
Turn out from here

Reverse

Stuff
Stuff Cotton

Front

Green thread

Front

Stuff with cotton and sew shut

**18**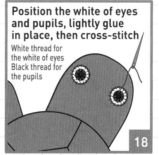
Position the white of eyes and pupils, lightly glue in place, then cross-stitch

White thread for the white of eyes
Black thread for the pupils

**19**
View from the top.

**Done**

View from the side.

# Turtlie Materials

- Glue
- Chalk pencils (Dark, Light)
- Cotton
- Scissors
- Sewing needle
- If you have one: Sewing machine
- Jersey cloth (Green)
- Stretch thread (Green)
- Felt (White, Black)
- Regular thread (White, Black)
- Pellets (Heavy, clear, grain-like packings)

# Turtlie Patterns

## Enlarge to 150% for the ideal size

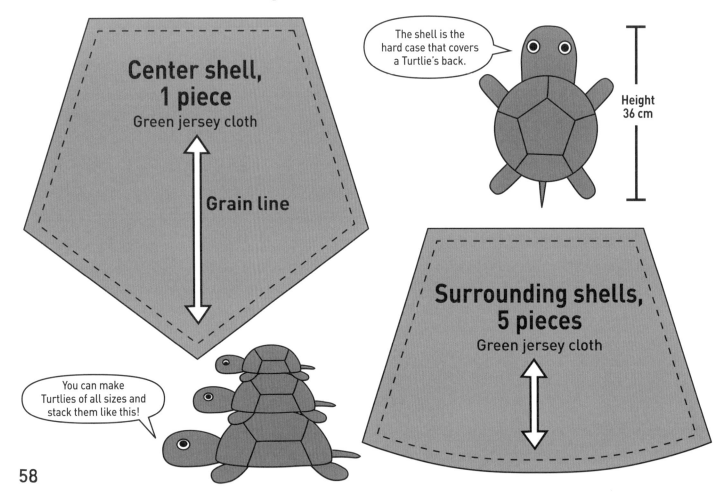

**Center shell, 1 piece**
Green jersey cloth

Grain line

The shell is the hard case that covers a Turtlie's back.

Height 36 cm

**Surrounding shells, 5 pieces**
Green jersey cloth

You can make Turtlies of all sizes and stack them like this!

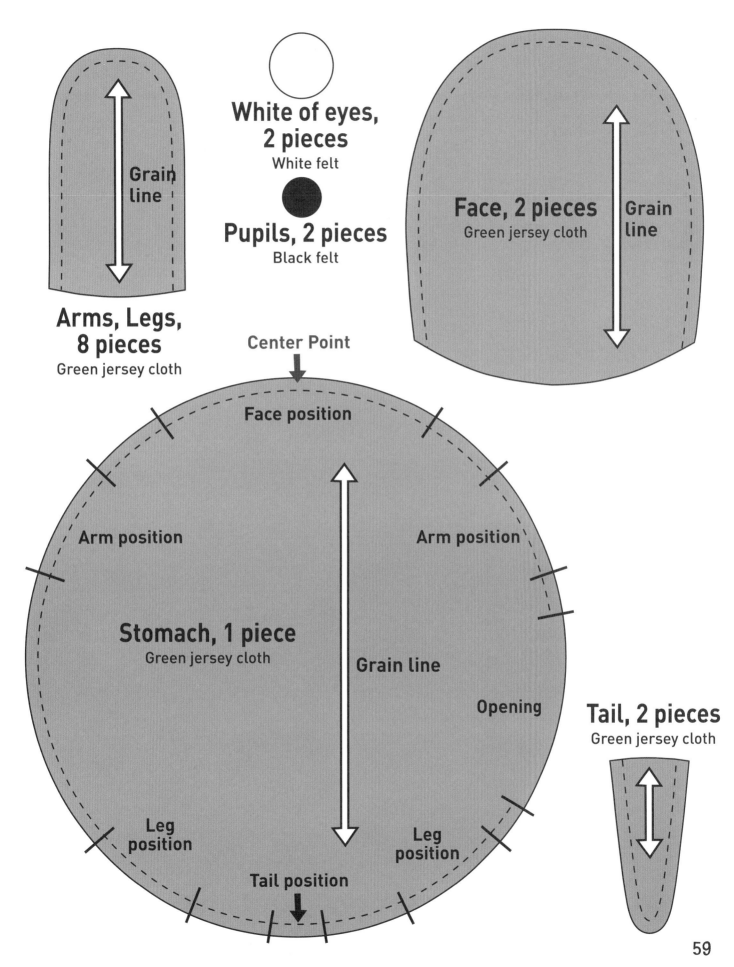

**Arms, Legs, 8 pieces**
Green jersey cloth

Grain line

**White of eyes, 2 pieces**
White felt

**Pupils, 2 pieces**
Black felt

**Face, 2 pieces**
Green jersey cloth

Grain line

Center Point

Face position

Arm position

Arm position

**Stomach, 1 piece**
Green jersey cloth

Grain line

Opening

Leg position

Leg position

Tail position

**Tail, 2 pieces**
Green jersey cloth

Beep beep! The speed limit's 40. Slow down!
Beep beep! I'm making a left turn, I'd better look both ways!
Beep beep! There's a stop sign. Watch out!
Beep beep! What NO ENTRY? Darn it!

# How to Make Car Folk

---

### 01
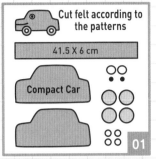
Cut felt according to the patterns

41.5 X 6 cm

Compact Car

### 02
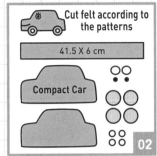
Cut felt according to the patterns

41.5 X 6 cm

Compact Car

### 03
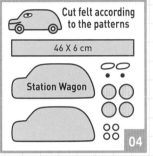
Cut felt according to the patterns

55.5 X 6 cm

Minivan

### 04
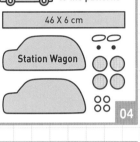
Cut felt according to the patterns

46 X 6 cm

Station Wagon

---

### 05
**The side piece is long. If you don't have felt that's long enough, sew separate pieces together**

① I don't have a piece of felt this long!

41.5 X 6 cm

② Make 3 shorter pieces

20 X 6 cm    20 X 6 cm    5.5 X 6 cm

③ Sew the pieces together to make one long piece

(Sew about 1 cm in)

Reverse

Front

Combine to make it 41.5 cm, though it doesn't have to be exactly 41.5 cm (longer is fine, but not shorter)

### 06
**Line up the Sewing Start Points of the car body and side with both pieces turned inside out**

Body
Sewing Start Point

about 0.5 cm in

about 1 cm in

Sewing Start Point
Side

### 07
**From the Sewing Start Point, sew along the dotted red line**

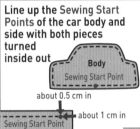

Reverse of body
Sewing Start Point
Reverse of side

Thread of felt's color

---

### 08
**Sew the other half of the body to the other side by lining up the Sewing Start Points and sewing along the dotted red line**

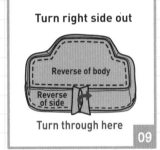

Reverse of body
Sewing Start Point
Reverse of side

### 09
**Turn right side out**

Reverse of body

Reverse of side

Turn through here

### 10
**Stuff with cotton**

Reverse of body
Front of side    Cotton

Front of body
Sew shut
Front of side

### 11
**Sew on the tires**

Thread can be any color

Sew tire's center firmly on body

---

### 12
**Lightly glue the hubcaps on the tire, then cross-stitch**

White thread

### 13
**Lightly glue the white of eyes and pupils in place, then cross-stitch**

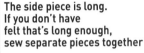

Black    Black

Draw the mouth with a pen

White thread for the white of eyes
Black thread for the pupils

Same goes for the other side

### 14
**Lightly glue the white of eyes and pupils in place, then cross-stitch**

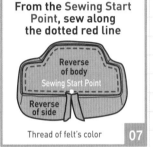

Black

White thread for the white of eyes
Black thread for the pupils

Draw the mouth and eyelashes with a pen

---

### 15
**Lightly glue the white of eyes, pupils, and three windows in place, then cross-stitch**

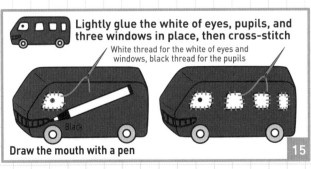

White thread for the white of eyes and windows, black thread for the pupils

Black

Draw the mouth with a pen

### 16
**Lightly glue the white of eyes and pupils in place, then cross-stitch**

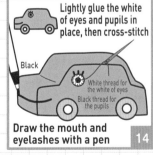

White thread for the white of eyes, black thread for the pupils

Black

Draw mouth with pen

### 17

**Done**

Have fun choosing colors, shapes, and faces!

# Car Folk Materials

- **Glue**
- **Chalk pencils** (Dark / Light)
- **Cotton**
- **Scissors**
- **Sewing needle**
- If you have one **Sewing machine**

**Felt**

| White | Gray | Black | Color of your choice |
|-------|------|-------|----------------------|

**Regular Thread**

- White
- Black
- Color of felt

**Pen** Cloth pen or Magic marker (Black)

---

**Minivan side, 1 piece**
Red felt
55.5 cm — 6 cm

**Station Wagon side, 1 piece**
Yellow felt
46 cm — 6 cm

> The side piece patterns are not at actual size. Please make the side pieces according to the dimensions specified.

**Compact Car side, 1 piece**
Blue felt
41.5 cm — 6 cm

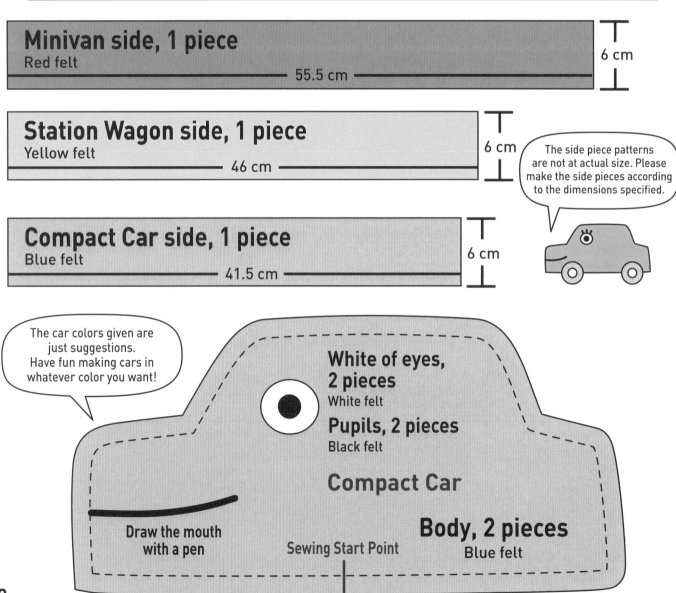

> The car colors given are just suggestions. Have fun making cars in whatever color you want!

**White of eyes, 2 pieces**
White felt

**Pupils, 2 pieces**
Black felt

**Compact Car**

**Body, 2 pieces**
Blue felt

Draw the mouth with a pen

Sewing Start Point

# Car Folk Patterns

**Pattern is at 100%, no need to enlarge
(but for the side pieces,
cut according to specified dimensions)**

**Hubcaps,
4 pieces**
White felt

**Tires,
4 pieces**
Gray felt

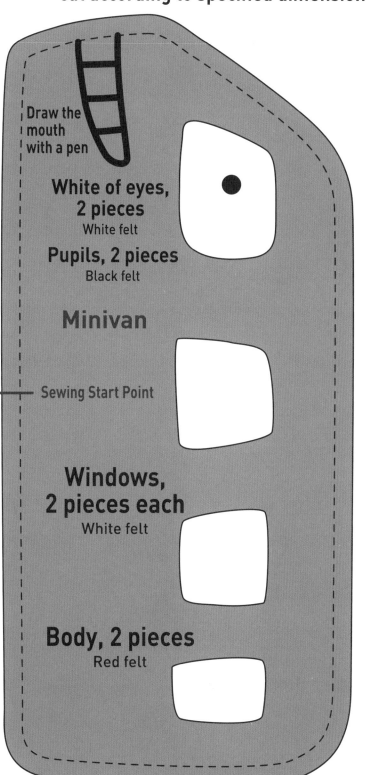

**Draw the
mouth
with a pen**

**White of eyes,
2 pieces**
White felt

**Pupils, 2 pieces**
Black felt

**Minivan**

Sewing Start Point

**Windows,
2 pieces each**
White felt

**Body, 2 pieces**
Red felt

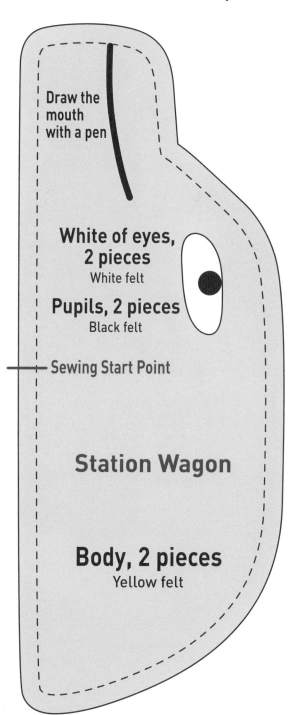

**Draw the
mouth
with a pen**

**White of eyes,
2 pieces**
White felt

**Pupils, 2 pieces**
Black felt

Sewing Start Point

**Station Wagon**

**Body, 2 pieces**
Yellow felt

Snakes have scary, big mouths.
But that's what makes them charming.
Snakes have scary, glaring eyes.
But that also adds to their charm.
Snakes show off their charm by hanging off
or coiling around things.

# How to Make Snakes

## Cut canvas cloth and red cotton fabric according to the patterns

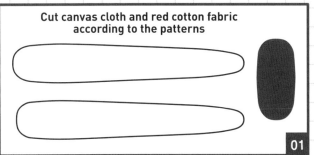

**01**

## Trace glaring eyes ⬭ and flowers ❋ onto erasers.

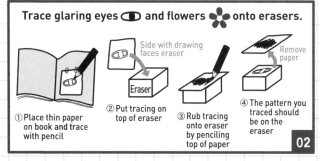

① Place thin paper on book and trace with pencil

② Put tracing on top of eraser

③ Rub tracing onto eraser by penciling top of paper

Side with drawing faces eraser

Remove paper

④ The pattern you traced should be on the eraser

**02**

## Using a razor or Exacto knife, cut around the traced patterns of the eye ⬭ and flower ❋ to make an eraser stamp

Cut off about 2 mm of the eraser so that the pattern is in relief

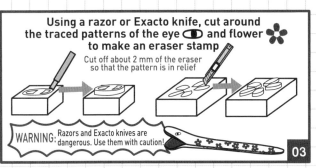

WARNING: Razors and Exacto knives are dangerous. Use them with caution!

**03**

## Test your eraser stamp on some scrap cloth

To make sure the stamp prints cleanly, test it several times on some scrap cloth

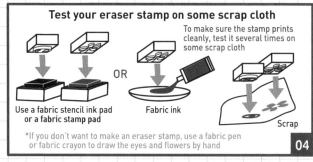

Use a fabric stencil ink pad or a fabric stamp pad

OR

Fabric ink

Scrap

*If you don't want to make an eraser stamp, use a fabric pen or fabric crayon to draw the eyes and flowers by hand

**04**

## Stamp the eyes ⬭ and flowers ❋ onto the body

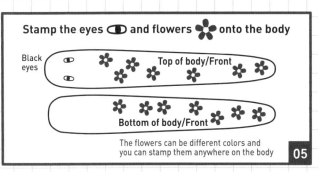

Black eyes

Top of body/Front

Bottom of body/Front

The flowers can be different colors and you can stamp them anywhere on the body

**05**

## Lining up the joints of the mouth and the ends of the tail, stack the halves of the body inside out and sew along the dotted red line

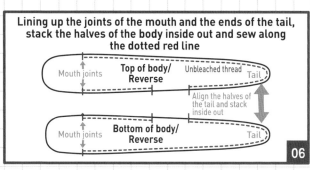

Mouth joints

Top of body/Reverse

Unbleached thread

Tail

Align the halves of the tail and stack inside out

Mouth joints

Bottom of body/Reverse

Tail

**06**

## Open wide the mouth joints (which should remain unsewn). Stack mouth and body, aligning mouth joints, tops of mouth and body, and bottoms of mouth and body

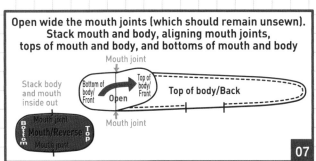

Stack body and mouth inside out

Bottom of body/Front

Open

Top of body/Front

Top of body/Back

Mouth joint

Mouth joint

Mouth/Reverse

Bottom

Top

Mouth joint

Mouth joint

**07**

## With the mouth and body aligned inside out, sew along the dotted red line

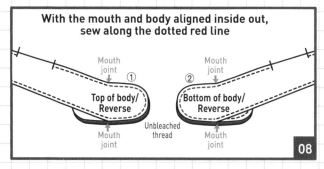

Mouth joint

① 

Top of body/Reverse

Mouth joint

Unbleached thread

Mouth joint

② 

Bottom of body/Reverse

Mouth joint

**08**

**Turn right side out through here**

① 

Reverse

Canvas cloth is tough hence difficult to turn out. Use a sharp object to pluck it right side out

**Once turned right side out, fill the body with pellets and sew shut**

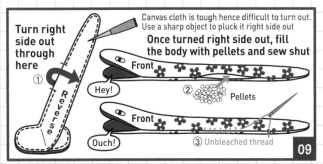

Front

Hey!

② 

Pellets

Front

Ouch!

③ Unbleached thread

**09**

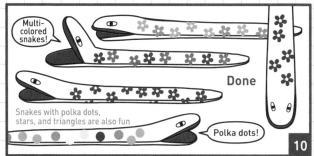

Multi-colored snakes!

Done

Snakes with polka dots, stars, and triangles are also fun

Polka dots!

**10**

# Snake Materials

- Glue
- Chalk pencils (Dark / Light)
- Pellets (Heavy, clear, grain-like packings)
- Scissors
- Sewing needle
- If you have one Sewing machine
- Light canvas cloth — Unbleached
- Regular Thread — Unbleached
- Cotton fabric — Red
- Awl
- Razor or Exacto knife **or** Box cutter
- Eraser
- Fabric stencil ink pad or stamp pad — Black / Color of flowers (color of your choice) **or** Fabric Ink — Black / Color of flowers **or** Magic marker — Black / Color of flower

# Snake Patterns

## Patterns for Eraser Stamps
### Actual size (do not enlarge)

Snake eyes

Flower

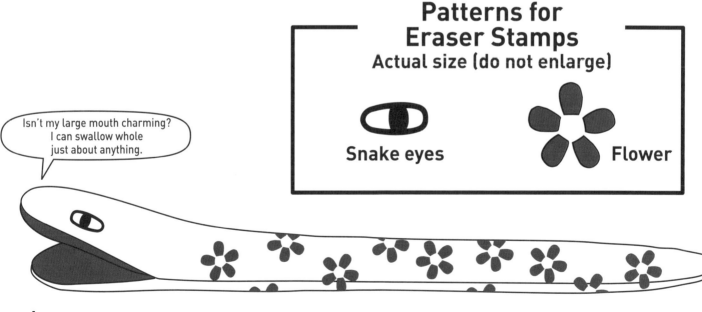

Isn't my large mouth charming? I can swallow whole just about anything.

Length when complete, 39 cm

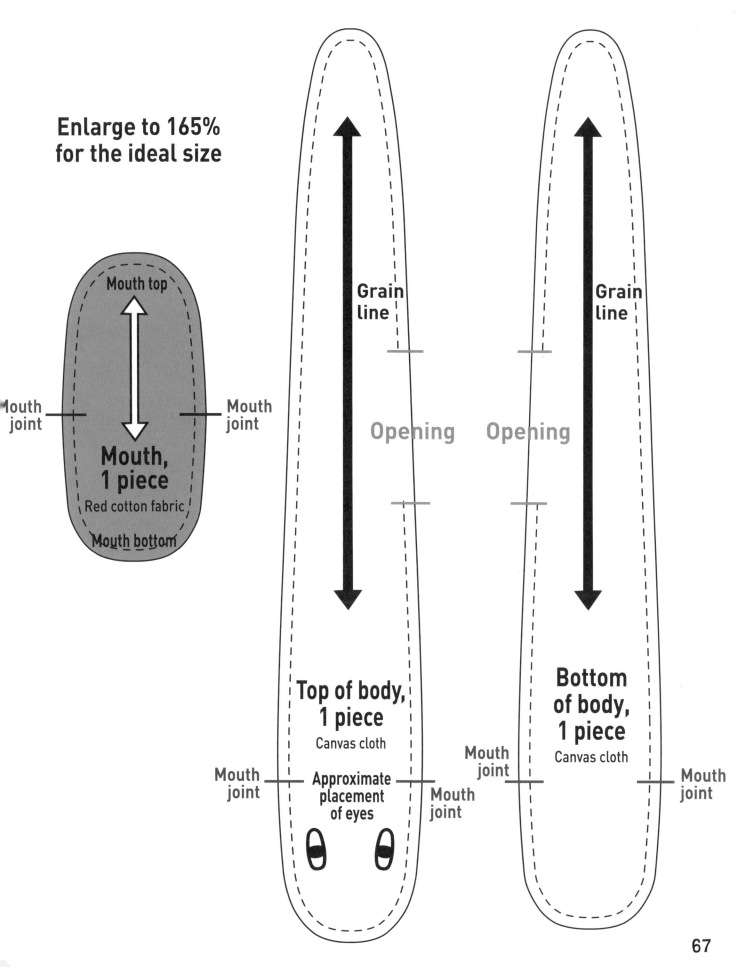

**Enlarge to 165% for the ideal size**

Mouth top

Mouth joint

Mouth joint

**Mouth, 1 piece**
Red cotton fabric

Mouth bottom

Grain line

Opening

Top of body, 1 piece
Canvas cloth

Mouth joint

Approximate placement of eyes

Mouth joint

Grain line

Opening

Mouth joint

**Bottom of body, 1 piece**
Canvas cloth

Mouth joint

Panda Bug will quietly listen to your problems.
Bunny Bug will politely laugh at your woeful jokes.
They can be used as cushions or pillows.
Living with these bugs will soothe your heart and heal your pain.

# How to Make Panda Bug and Bunny Bug

## 01

Cut Panda Bug terry cloth according to the patterns

Cut Panda Bug felt according to the patterns

## 02
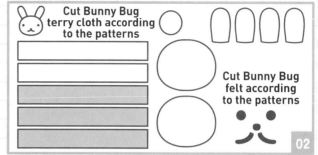
Cut Bunny Bug terry cloth according to the patterns

Cut Bunny Bug felt according to the patterns

## 03
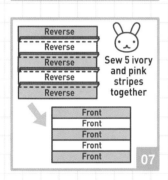
Stack the ears inside out and sew along the dotted white line

Black thread
Reverse
Reverse
Front
Cotton
Turn right side out
Stuff with cotton

## 04
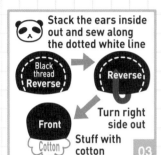
Stack the ears inside out and sew along the dotted red line

Stuff with cotton

Unbleached thread
Reverse
Reverse
Front
Cotton
Turn right side out

## 05

Stack different colored stripes inside out and sew along the dotted red line

White thread
Reverse
White
Black
Unbleached thread
Reverse
Ivory
Pink

## 06
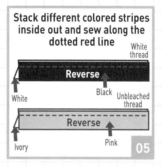
Reverse
Reverse
Reverse
Reverse
Reverse
Sew 5 black and white stripes together

Front
Front
Front
Front
Front

## 07
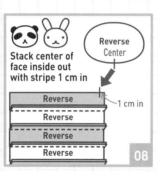
Reverse
Reverse
Reverse
Reverse
Reverse
Sew 5 ivory and pink stripes together

Front
Front
Front
Front
Front

## 08

Stack center of face inside out with stripe 1 cm in

Reverse Center

Reverse
Reverse
Reverse
1 cm in

## 09
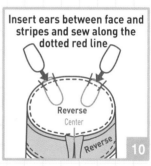
Reverse Center

White thread
Unbleached thread

Sew face and stripes around the edge, repeat with bottom (Do not sew over the ear positions)
Tack before you sew

## 10
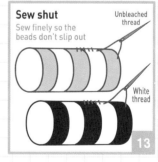
Insert ears between face and stripes and sew along the dotted red line

Reverse Center
Reverse

## 11
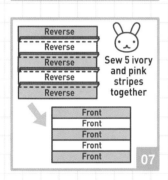
White thread
Unbleached thread

Sew along the dotted red line of the stripes. Leave about 8 cm open in the middle

Leave about 8 cm open

Center
Reverse of face
Reverse
Reverse of bottom

## 12
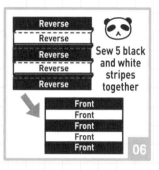
Stuff with foam beads
These beads are small and fluffy, so you'll need a funnel

Fluff Fluff Fluff Fluff

Wide opening

Roll up a piece of paper

Narrow opening

Insert the narrow end into the stripes' opening and pour foam beads into the wide end

## 13

Sew shut
Sew finely so the beads don't slip out

Unbleached thread
White thread

## 14
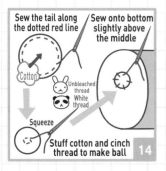
Sew the tail along the dotted red line / Sew onto bottom slightly above the middle

Cotton
Unbleached thread
White thread
Squeeze
Stuff cotton and cinch thread to make ball

## 15
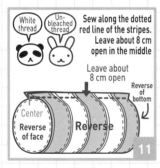
Position eyes, nose, and mouth, glue lightly in place, then cross-stitch

Black thread.

## 16

Position eyes, nose, and mouth, glue lightly in place, then cross-stitch

Brown thread.

## 17

Done
They're happy you made them

# Panda Bug and Bunny Bug Materials

 Glue

**Chalk pencils** Dark Light

 **Scissors**

**Sewing needle**

If you have one **Sewing machine**

**Terry cloth**

White | Black | Ivory (A slightly yellowish white) | Pink

**Felt**

Black | Brown

**Regular Thread**

Black | White | Brown | Unbleached

**Foam Beads** (Styrofoam)
Small Styrofoam beads are nice because they add a funky texture

If you don't have Styrofoam, you can use cotton
Cotton
Cotton is nice because your doll will be soft like a cushion

# Panda Bug and Bunny Bug Patterns

## Pattern is at 100%, no need to enlarge

**Eyes, 2 pieces**
Black felt

 **Eyes, 2 pieces**
Brown felt

 **Nose, 1 piece**
Brown felt

 **Right mouth, 1 piece**
Brown felt

**Left mouth, 1 piece**
Brown felt

 **Nose, 1 piece**
Black felt

 **Right mouth, 1 piece**
Black felt

 **Left mouth, 1 piece**
Black felt

9 cm

Approx. 53 cm

**Note: This pattern is not to scale. Please make the pattern according to the dimensions indicated.**

 **Stripe, 2 pieces**
White terry cloth

**Stripe, 3 pieces**
Black terry cloth

 **Stripe, 2 pieces**
Ivory terry cloth

 **Stripe, 3 pieces**
Pink terry cloth

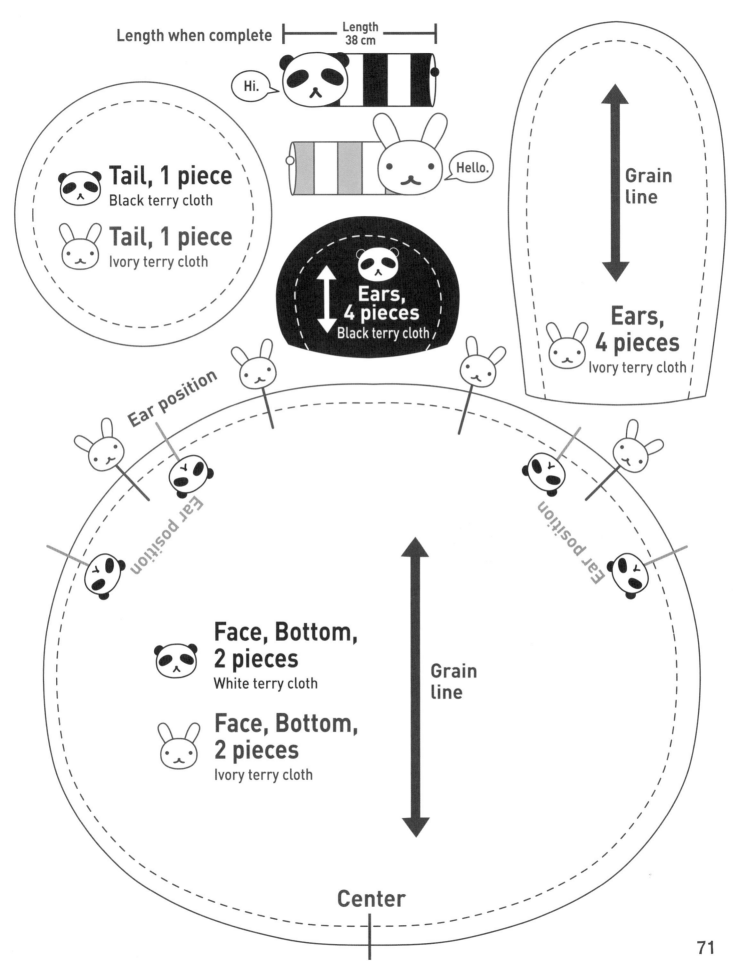

Length when complete — Length 38 cm

Hi.

Hello.

Tail, 1 piece
Black terry cloth

Tail, 1 piece
Ivory terry cloth

Ears, 4 pieces
Black terry cloth

Grain line

Ears, 4 pieces
Ivory terry cloth

Ear position

Ear position

Ear position

Ear position

Face, Bottom, 2 pieces
White terry cloth

Face, Bottom, 2 pieces
Ivory terry cloth

Grain line

Center

You can't drink tea out of these mugs.
They'll just get soggy.
But if you place them on a table like this, they look kind of cool.
You can make various Coffee Mugs and line them up.
That would look kind of cool, too.

# How to Make Coffee Mugs

## 01
**Cut a fabric of your choice according to the patterns**

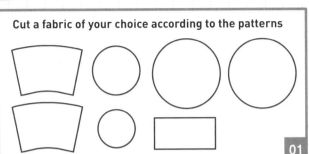

## 02
**Cut the facial expression of your choice out of felt according to the patterns**
You can make a facial expression that's not in the Patterns, too

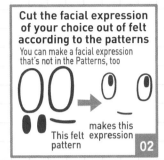

This felt pattern → makes this expression

## 03
**Stack the side pieces of the Coffee Mug inside out and sew along the dotted red line**

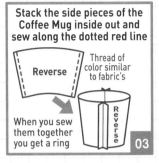

Reverse — Thread of color similar to fabric's

When you sew them together you get a ring

## 04
Top of Coffee Mug — Connection points

① **Connect the top and side inside out at the red arrows**

② **Tack around the top piece from the red arrows** (a straight stitch to keep it in place will be sufficient)

③ **After you've tacked the top piece, sew by machine or hand along the dotted red line, then pull out the tacking thread**

Reverse of Coffee Mug side

Sew about 0.5 cm in

Sew about 1 cm in

Pull

The final stitch will be neater if you tack first!

## 05
**Sew on the bottom piece of Coffee Mug the same way you sewed the top piece**

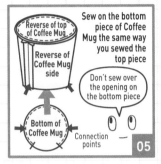

Reverse of top of Coffee Mug

Reverse of Coffee Mug side

Don't sew over the opening on the bottom piece

Bottom of Coffee Mug

Connection points

## 06
**Turn Coffee Mug right side out through the opening**

Reverse of top of Coffee Mug

Reverse of Coffee Mug side

Turn out from here

## 07
**Stuff with cotton and sew shut**

Front of top of Coffee Mug

Front of Coffee Mug side

Front of bottom of Coffee Mug

Stuff · Cotton · Stuff

## 08
**Fold the handle in half inside out and sew along the dotted red line**

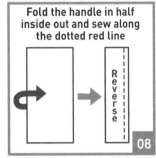

Reverse

## 09
**Turn right side out**

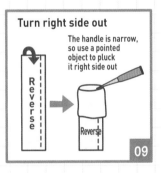

The handle is narrow, so use a pointed object to pluck it right side out

Reverse

## 10
**Stuff with cotton from top and bottom**

The handle is narrow so use a thin, stick-like object to stuff

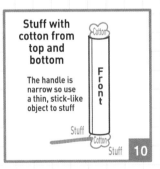

Cotton · Front · Cotton · Stuff

## 11
① **Bend the handle now stuffed with cotton**
② **Fold in about 1 cm at each end**
③ **Sew onto the side**

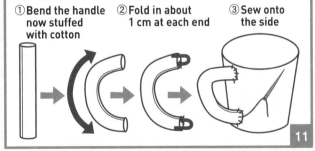

## 12
**Stack the two saucer pieces inside out and sew along the dotted red line**

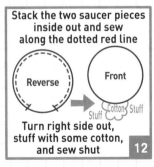

Reverse — Front

Stuff · Cotton · Stuff

Turn right side out, stuff with some cotton, and sew shut

## 13
**Position the eyes and mouth and glue in place**

Glue

Brown thread

If you're worried the face will fall off, cross-stitch into place

## 14
**Put the eyes and nose on the other side of the cup if you're left handed**

## 15

**Place Coffee Mug on its saucer and you're done**

You can make all kinds of Coffee Mugs

# Coffee Mug Materials

Glue

Chalk pencils — Dark, Light

Cotton

Scissors

Sewing needle

If you have one
Sewing machine

**Fabric of your choice**
In color or pattern of your choice

With stretchable, use **Stretch thread**
With non-stretchable, use **Regular thread**
Color similar to the fabric

**Felt** — Brown

**Regular thread** — Brown

**Awl** (Handy for turning Coffee Mug's handle right side out)

**Stick-like object** (Handy for stuffing the handle with cotton)

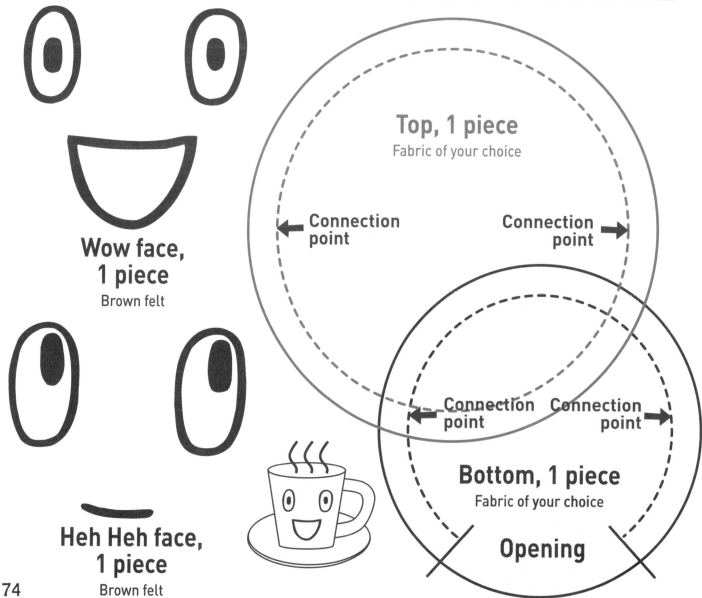

**Wow face, 1 piece**
Brown felt

**Heh Heh face, 1 piece**
Brown felt

**Top, 1 piece**
Fabric of your choice

← Connection point

Connection point →

Connection point

Connection point

**Bottom, 1 piece**
Fabric of your choice

**Opening**

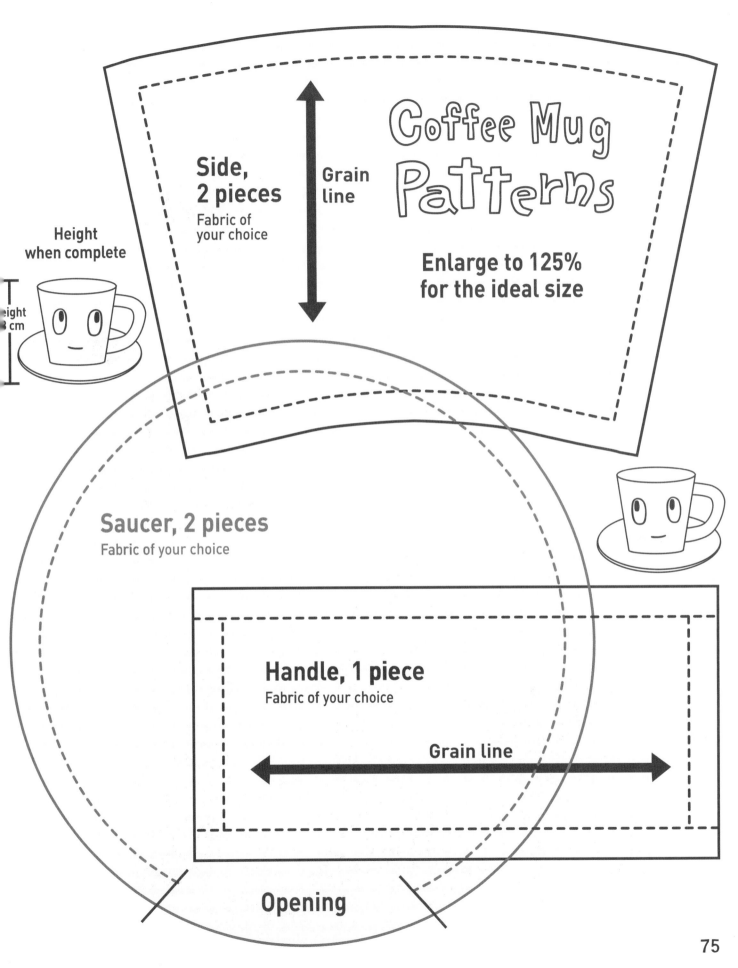

# Coffee Mug Patterns

**Side, 2 pieces**
Fabric of your choice

Grain line

Enlarge to 125% for the ideal size

Height when complete

eight
cm

**Saucer, 2 pieces**
Fabric of your choice

**Handle, 1 piece**
Fabric of your choice

Grain line

Opening

"Terry, can I lean on you for a while?"
"Ruff course! Having a ruff day?"
"Not really. I just want to lean on you."
"You're weird, ruff."

# How to Make Terry

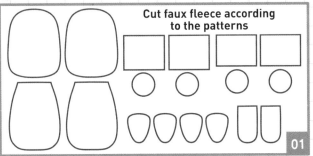

**Cut faux fleece according to the patterns**

01

**Cut felt according to the patterns**

Ruff.

02

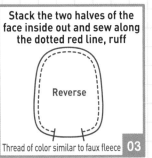

**Stack the two halves of the face inside out and sew along the dotted red line, ruff**

Reverse

Thread of color similar to faux fleece

03

**Turn right side out and stuff with cotton before sewing shut, ruff**

Reverse · Front · Front

Stuff Cotton Stuff

04

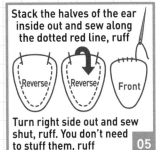

**Stack the halves of the ear inside out and sew along the dotted red line, ruff**

Reverse · Reverse · Front

**Turn right side out and sew shut, ruff. You don't need to stuff them, ruff**

05

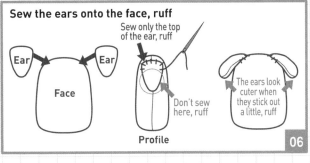

**Sew the ears onto the face, ruff**

Sew only the top of the ear, ruff

Ear · Face · Ear

Don't sew here, ruff

The ears look cuter when they stick out a little, ruff

Profile

06

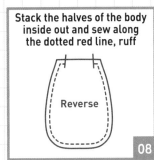

**Position the eyes, nose, and mouth, ruff Lightly glue in place, then cross-stitch, ruff**

Black thread

07

**Stack the halves of the body inside out and sew along the dotted red line, ruff**

Reverse

08

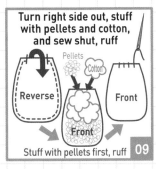

**Turn right side out, stuff with pellets and cotton, and sew shut, ruff**

Pellets · Cotton

Reverse · Front · Front

Stuff with pellets first, ruff

09

**Sew the face onto the body, ruff**

Front view · Rear view

10

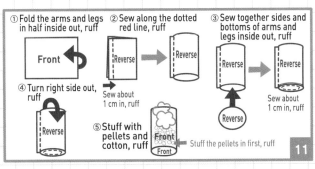

① Fold the arms and legs in half inside out, ruff

Front

② Sew along the dotted red line, ruff

Reverse · Reverse

③ Sew together sides and bottoms of arms and legs inside out, ruff

Reverse · Reverse

④ Turn right side out, ruff

Reverse

Sew about 1 cm in, ruff

⑤ Stuff with pellets and cotton, ruff

Reverse · Front · Front

Stuff the pellets in first, ruff

Sew about 1 cm in, ruff

11

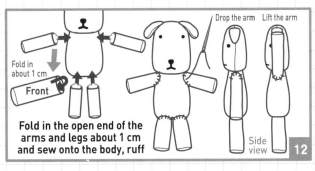

Drop the arm · Lift the arm

Fold in about 1 cm

Front

**Fold in the open end of the arms and legs about 1 cm and sew onto the body, ruff**

Side view

12

Reverse · Cotton · Front

**Stack the halves of the tail inside out and sew along the dotted red line, ruff Turn right side out and fill with pellets and cotton, ruff Sew onto the backside, ruff**

13

**Terry is not a white dog, so make his ears brown with a brown fabric ink pad or marker, ruff**

14

**Terry is not a white dog, so make his back black with a black fabric ink pad or marker, ruff**

Back

15

I'm Terry. I can sit, ruff.

**Done, ruff**

Terry the Aranzi Aronzo store dog, ruff

16

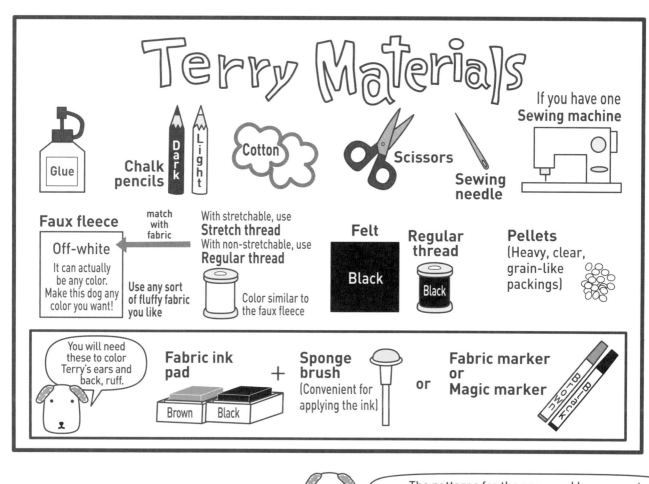

# Terry Materials

**Glue**

**Chalk pencils** — Dark, Light

**Cotton**

**Scissors**

**Sewing needle**

If you have one **Sewing machine**

**Faux fleece**
Off-white
It can actually be any color. Make this dog any color you want!

match with fabric

Use any sort of fluffy fabric you like

With stretchable, use **Stretch thread**
With non-stretchable, use **Regular thread**

Color similar to the faux fleece

**Felt** Black

**Regular thread** Black

**Pellets**
(Heavy, clear, grain-like packings)

You will need these to color Terry's ears and back, ruff.

**Fabric ink pad** — Brown, Black

+

**Sponge brush**
(Convenient for applying the ink)

or

**Fabric marker or Magic marker**

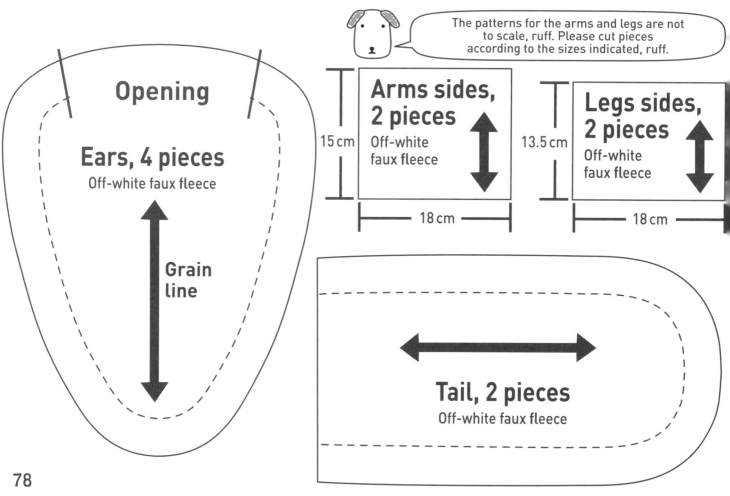

The patterns for the arms and legs are not to scale, ruff. Please cut pieces according to the sizes indicated, ruff.

**Opening**

**Ears, 4 pieces**
Off-white faux fleece

Grain line

**Arms sides, 2 pieces**
Off-white faux fleece
15 cm × 18 cm

**Legs sides, 2 pieces**
Off-white faux fleece
13.5 cm × 18 cm

**Tail, 2 pieces**
Off-white faux fleece

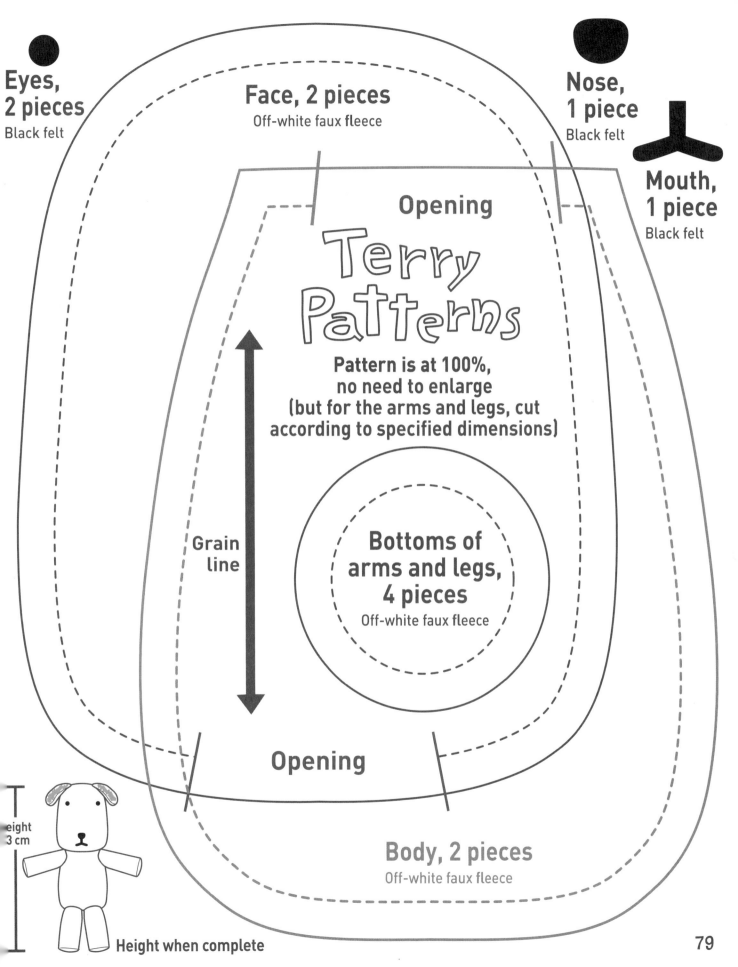

**Eyes,
2 pieces**
Black felt

**Face, 2 pieces**
Off-white faux fleece

**Nose,
1 piece**
Black felt

**Mouth,
1 piece**
Black felt

Opening

# Terry Patterns

**Pattern is at 100%,
no need to enlarge
(but for the arms and legs, cut
according to specified dimensions)**

Grain
line

**Bottoms of
arms and legs,
4 pieces**
Off-white faux fleece

Opening

**Body, 2 pieces**
Off-white faux fleece

Height
3 cm

**Height when complete**

**ARANZI ARONZO**

Aranzi Aronzo is a company that
"makes what it feels like the way it feels like and then sells the stuff."
Established in 1991 in Osaka. Kinuyo Saito and Yoko Yomura team.
Other than original miscellany, Aranzi Aronzo also makes picture books and exhibits.
Other books include *The Cute Book, The Bad Book, Aranzi Machine Gun vols. 1-3, Cute Dolls* and *Cute Stuff.*

http://www.aranziaronzo.com
http://www.vertical-inc.com/aranzi_aronzo

Translation — Anne Ishii

Copyright © 2007 by Aranzi Aronzo

All rights reserved.

Published by Vertical, Inc., New York.

Originally published in Japanese as *Iroiro nuigurumi*
by Bunka Shuppankyoku, Tokyo, 2003.

ISBN 978-1-932234-79-4

Manufactured in Singapore

Second Printing

Vertical, Inc.
www.vertical-inc.com